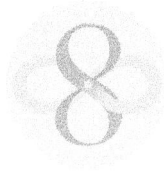

International Praise for this Book

In *Getting There by Being Here*, Angela Silva Mendes encourages us to slow down and participate whole-heartedly in the dynamic flow of life, which is more than just one endless, self-improvement project. Through personal stories and innovative invitations to self-inquiry, Angela writes and shares from her own direct experience and realizations, which have been hard won, embodied fruits of her own journey through the darkness and into the light of compassionate awareness.

—Matt Licata, PhD
Author of A Healing Space: Befriending Ourselves
in Difficult Times *and* The Path is Everywhere:
Discovering the Jewels Hidden Within You
Colorado, USA

In this book Angela shared what she has learned to put into practice. I met Angela many years ago, just at the right time. I was a foreigner in a country where I was almost alone, newlywed, and a little bit scared of my new life. She then appeared as a soft breeze with her sweet voice, always willing to help. She was there in a very tough time and then she danced with me through the pain, giving me her time and kindness, and that made it easier to endure my loss. That was her mission in my life, and as she helped me, she did it with so many people. All of those who were around her knew what her mission was, and I'm so glad to have been part of her journey of giving her soul to help others. Let's dance through her beautiful words, thoughts, and experiences written by a wonderful dancer.

—Gaby Cantero
Radio Locutor at Super 98.9 F.M.
Colima, Mexico

Rare is the book that engages you so magnetically in the story of the author and her clients, and through these stories illuminates "life's invitations to dance." Angela offers the reader a tantalizing view into how she explored the first steps of her own life's choreography and surrendered to the flow of our essential nature that is energy. Angela offers the reader opportunities for self-exploration through *Homeplay*, an invitation to be curious, turn inward and surrender to the melody within. In the process, the reader is unraveled and healed. An excellent addition for my self-help shelf.

—Pami Loomba
Lawyer, Human Rights Activist and Life Coach
Manchester, England

This book is a do-it-yourself manual on personal development informed by spirituality. Using the metaphor of dance, Angela playfully leads us through beautifully crafted chapters inviting us to explore our self-limiting beliefs and resistance to change. She illustrates through examples from her own life and the experiences of her clients what acceptance and progress looks like. This way of looking at life—as a continuous, flowing dance—provides a key insight that life is very much a process of curious, open engagement rather than a linear progression where every setback is something to be judged and stored away for future reference. Written in a deceptively simple style, the book draws on a wide sweep of knowledge and understanding of the human condition. It pulls together many different techniques, concepts, and insights, gently holding the reader's hand and demonstrating what the dance might look like in different situations. I highly recommend you accept this invitation despite any discomfort of tight shoes and bright lights that may arise, because forming a deeper relation with that discomfort is precisely the intention of this book!

—Lalita Ramesh
Environmentalist, Tai Chi Instructor
Connecticut, USA

The writing style is beautiful—very engaging and takes you "in" as if Angela was sitting here talking to you. The way that she shares the stories is informative and, at the same time, you learn something while reading them without really realizing it. I love the *Homeplay* sections—for me, this is an important part of a book where we can physically engage with it, so we are looking at the movement of dance as the theme and then physically doing something—I really like that. As someone who has done a lot of work on myself and still continually do, it inspired me and helped me to see a few things differently as well. The way I engage with things and embrace the fluidity of them is a nice one for me, as I can be quite tough and hard on myself, so this was a nice touch that I needed to read. I would highly recommend this for anyone who is facing change of some sort—it's a challenging time for anyone, but the approach is light and fluid and I really like that.

—Gareth Stubbs
Co-Author of Inside Out, The Big Mindful Colorful Book, *and* Fuel
Co-Founder and Co-Owner of Inside Out Spain, D-Toxd Living
Founder of the Vegan Food Company
Spain

If you can't work with Angela as your life coach, then this book really is the next best thing. It's a portable guide to living your best life, one of integrity and purpose. The book provides a road map that brings you right back to your true self, helping you create the life you know deep down is best for you. Angela's approach is nonjudgemental and extremely effective. Her philosophy of keeping the end in mind while staying deeply focused on the present moment has helped me to create great change in my life. I highly recommend her work.

—Candace Walt
Teacher
Portugal

Angela uses the "Bus Ride" to illustrate that being present in the moment provides possibilities to experience life differently—more fully and deeply. Being present means letting go of our cultural, familial, or personal pre-conditioning to experience "what is" instead of "what should be" and that life can be lived as a Dance. Angela's expert guidance allows us—clients and readers—to Dance through life's joys and challenges.

—Akke Hulburts
Yoga teacher, Structural Yoga Therapist and Massage Therapist
Virginia, USA

The author, Angela Silva Mendes, claims that "there are no secret strategies to get you there nor any magic tricks." Life is truly about being present. This is the reason to get interested in this topic: life's invitation to dance. It is so clear and beautiful. The life experience examples shared are easy to relate to. The reflections on how one can change focus to change the feeling of anxiety is so well explained. It triggered me to stop and reflect on how I would have behaved or reacted if it was happening to me. The language in this book is well written, it is clear, and visuals came automatically. Despite the fact that English is not my native language, I had no problem reading it with ease and delight. It is truly a gift.

—Jeanette Nerlinger
Interior Architect MNIL
Oslo, Norway

I looked for Angela at a time when I needed to focus my attention and determination on my professional life. The first session where we did the "deathbed" exercise was enough to be absolutely convinced that I was choosing the right person to help me. We did intensive work for about two years, after which I managed to put my ideas on paper, eventually materializing it in my business, in my art, and my passion. With Angela we learn to look inside, to listen to our hearts, to tame our impulses, and to end our bad habits. My profession and company have been set up in the last 10 years, but it is the individual person in me who has benefited most from this investment. The learnings I got from Angela got into me and stayed for the rest of my life. Our work was so important and continues to have a positive impact in my life. I can't wait to have this book in my hands to reread it as many times needed and remember everything that Angela taught me and offer it to so many people to whom I have already recommended Angela.

—Marta Champalimaud
Founder of the clothing brand Martine Love
Lisbon, Portugal

Angela Mendes invites us all to become closer to ourselves and to create our own dance. The idea is that one can open themselves up just a little bit more. She invites us to explore and encourages us to be curious, to play, and to be present. She connects us through her own personal experiences and provides us with opportunities to grow in our own way and in the timeline we set for ourselves. We learn how "to be" in an experience, to zoom in and zoom out while shifting our decision making to one that is supportive and accepting. This piece of wisdom is calling for you to read it. Utilize the practices that resonate with you and begin to bring a greater acceptance of life's beautiful invitations into your daily world.

—Kimberly Fleck
Author, Creative, and Storyteller
Connecticut, USA

Since meeting Angela a few years ago, I often thought how useful it would be to have her insights and guidance down on paper. The wait is over! *Getting There by Being Here* is a down-to-earth guide for knowing the self, the true self—not the idealized versions of who we think we ought to be, but who we really are. The book is an invitation for us as individuals to come home to ourselves, our path, our calling in life, through learning to accept "Life's invitations to dance," stay open and present to the trials and tribulations that life will inevitably throw our way, and be willing to change course as many times as is necessary. In candidly sharing her own unconventional path to the work that she does, Angela demonstrates that your life may not turn out as you had planned but may well be exactly what you need.

—Elizabeth O'Hagan
Yoga Teacher
Belfast, Northern Ireland

Angela Mendes has created a compassionate companion to living life in the now with love and grace. Her meditative guidance to visualize my Deathbed opened an inspiring imaginary conversation with the older version of me, thereby awakening a whole new confident sense of self to experience peace within the present. Angela's practices, as described in this book, helped me realize that all the wisdom I had wanted already existed within. *Getting There by Being Here* is a joyful and supportive read for anyone desiring to dance with conscious authenticity.

—Fiona Dawson
Executive Producer & Creator, NOW with Fiona
freelionproductions.com
Austin, Texas, USA

One big value of the book is the profound honesty of writing, the generosity in telling and in giving courage. There are no filters on the author's past wounds and doubts, but the authenticity makes everything very gentle. The metaphor of the dance is very effective, easy to understand, and, recalling a physical experience, easy to imagine also in a mental practice. It makes you want to accept the invitation because everyone can do it without steps to learn and without judgment since "I can only dance as I am." I loved that in the direct and energetic style of this book there is no space for words like "difficult, fear, problem," but practice is the key word, no mental training, and everyone can try and accept themselves and reality. The content of this book can help people develop awareness of the big tricks of our mind about control of life with thoughts. It is a great opportunity for freedom, and you see in the book how dance can give new colours and taste to life. I really appreciate the introduction and offer of the experience in Mozambique; this is a brilliant and encouraging example in changing focus. The story is told in a tragicomic mixed mode, and lets people understand that everyone has the opportunity, the "tools," and the insights to do it. This story is to show everyone, with great humility, that it is possible, if you try, to make choices without turning your head away from the present. The *Homeplay* is the link to our identity and experience and is very important. It could be the hook to overcome the embarrassment of the beginning of the practice.

—Anna Bertelli
History of Art, Ceramist and Ceramic Restorer, www.annabertelli.it
Bologna, Italy

Angela's writing is deeply eye- and mind-opening. I highly recommend her book to anyone who wants to find more depth and satisfaction in their life and relationships. Angela's insights planted some very powerful seeds into me. These started to grow and blossom, taking my life into a very positive direction where I feel empowered to create the life of my dreams. At the beginning it was not easy, as her approach is radically different from the practices I've come in contact with so far. Yet it's precisely her radical simplicity that I love! I greatly appreciate her putting her work into print form, so that I am able to come back to it over and over again. At the same time, I highly recommend working with her one-on-one. Her clarity helped pierce through my resistances and showed me change is easier than I had expected.

—Masha Kovacs
Yoga, Feldenkrais, Embodied Awareness, Functional Bodywork
Innsbruck, Austria

It's a book full of direct human-based experiences and the way we get tangled up in being somewhere else and how mindfulness can support us in being right here. It feels very vibrant, and Angela's expertise bringing it all to the dance just speaks so directly to the connection we all have and are in and through these bodies. I celebrate the language and the intensity, the enthusiasm, and Angela's wise guidance.

—Karen Sevenoff
American Folk Artist
Connecticut, USA

I was captivated right away by the book's honesty and how familiar it felt. I like how Angela pays attention to how different we are from each other and takes that into consideration. Life is constantly changing, and we should learn to dance our way in. Knowing what kind of tools I can use isn't enough sometimes, and while I was reading I could find new ways of using certain tools to help myself in my day-to-day life. As someone who struggles with addiction, that chapter hit right home, and I could feel inspired after reading it. Most of the time these kinds of health/spiritual books just give you the tools without showing you how to use them, which is why this book is so refreshing as it actually shows different ways of using those tools.

—Anne Lia
Goldsmith, Veterinarian
Portugal

I couldn't put the book down, and I'd recommend it to anyone interested in navigating the twists and turns in the dance of life. A dance across a dancefloor is never linear. The dance moves left, right, forwards, and backwards with many twists and turns. And so it is with life. In this book, Angela captures this essence through case studies and glimpses into her own life's dance. In particular, "You create your own reality" is a well-used phrase but it's hard to reconcile when experiencing hard times. My aha moment reading this book was that whilst we assume the experiences in life that move us around the dancefloor are exterior to us, it's the way that we react that matters most. How we react to an experience is how we create our reality. An obstacle in life is just an experience we perceive as having a negative impact on our life, and Angela provides four guiding principles to move around them.

—Yvonne Smith, PhD
EFT (Tapping) Coach
Manchester, England, UK

GETTING THERE
BY
BEING HERE

GETTING THERE
BY
BEING HERE

LIFE'S INVITATIONS TO DANCE

ANGELA SILVA MENDES

PYP

PUBLISH
YOUR
PURPOSE
PRESS

For permission requests, write to the publisher, addressed "Attention: Permissions Coordinator," at the address below.

Publish Your Purpose Press
141 Weston Street, #155
Hartford, CT, 06141

PUBLISH
YOUR
PURPOSE
PRESS

The opinions expressed by the Author are not necessarily those held by Publish Your Purpose Press.

Ordering Information: Quantity sales and special discounts are available on quantity purchases by corporations, associations, and others. For details, contact the publisher at orders@publishyourpurposepress.com.

Edited by: Gail Marlene Schwartz, Erin Walton, and Nancy Graham-Tillman
Cover Designed by Nelly Murariu
Typeset by: Medlar Publishing Solutions Pvt Ltd., India

Printed in the United States of America.
ISBN: 978-1-951591-55-7 (paperback)
ISBN: 978-1-951591-56-4 (ebook)

Library of Congress Control Number: 2021909750

First edition, June 2021.

V.1a

Publish Your Purpose Press works with authors, and aspiring authors, who have a story to tell and a brand to build. Do you have a book idea you would like us to consider publishing? Please visit PublishYourPurposePress. com for more information.

Disclaimer

I am an unconventional coach, an existentialist who values authenticity and believes in the uniqueness of each human as an integral part of nature. It is therefore the responsibility of each one of us to give meaning to our reality and to create the action required in each moment. At the same time, I also defend that as mammals, we exist in community and are embedded in the intersectionality of the collective unconscious. The movement of integration, between inner and outer, is the dance. Life is a dance, not a goal to reach a journey's destination. Life is ever- changing, with alternating directions, twists, and turns. As a life coach, I do not prescribe nor dictate moves for any other person's dance. *Here*, you will not find the industrialized systems to remove the undesirable or transform nature. There are no secret strategies to get you there nor any magic tricks.

I imagine myself as an organic farmer who respects and accepts nature and therefore learns to work with nature while continuing to create and produce. Similar to the movie

The Biggest Little Farm, I am faced with a curiosity guided by a core value. For when storms arrive, the soil is rich and strong to withstand the damages. Tending-to is never-ending work; hence I view it as a practice that every day requires us to take the pulse of the inner and outer conditions and take a step accordingly. In this book, I am inviting you to join me in this practice of getting closer to yourself *here*, which is a moment of rest. What I share stands on the work done by many as well as my own extensive and diverse educational and professional background. I will use "I" in recognition that what I see is influenced by who I am. Throughout the book, I will also use "we," but rest assured I am not assuming I know your experience; I am including myself in the struggle I see with many clients in my practice. If what I am referring to as "we" does not reflect your experience, please know I do respect and value your unique experience.

The practice *getting there by being here* is simple, but not always easy. Start where you are, as you are, with what is happening now, for these are life's invitations to dance. Once I noticed that *here* there is energy in me, I started inviting my clients to practice, and I delight in seeing them rest in their own rhythm. The stories shared are suggestions for you to practice, never a fixed set of rules. I trust you will find your own moves, for there is nothing like your own being *here*.

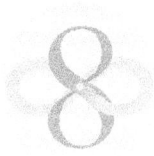

Dedication

*To my clients and the brave souls
who venture into the most beautiful and scary work and
who embrace the adventure of getting to know oneself.*

Acknowledgements

To my father and mother, thank you for being proud of me and for giving me the privilege of playing with opposites from a young age. To my sisters, there is not enough gratitude in this world for all you have given me. This book is also your work, for without you, I would not have the ground to be myself. To my nieces, nephew, and grandnephews, thank you for teaching me unconditional love.

To my best friend, partner, and husband, thank you for loving me no matter what. I thank my extended family for being there for us. I am blessed with friends who became family, and many around the world who enrich my life by allowing me to be part of theirs.

My grateful recognition for the many teachers and mentors in my life: authors, co-workers, teachers, peers, students, volunteers, and strangers with whom I converse. Each encounter is a piece of my ability to face the dance.

I am grateful for my clients' courage to see themselves, for they remind me about the power of life's dance. Thank you for your kind words, for recommending my work, for sharing testimonials, and above all, for giving me the privilege to be a part of your most amazing adventure into yourself.

A special *Namaste* to my game changers, the teachers, coaches, and therapists who support me: Evelyne Bozonet, Jules Wyman, Jeff Foster, Matt Licata, Liana Netto, and Sherry Osadchey. It has been a true gift to work with you and experience the field where love is the healer.

I want to name my most beautiful cheerleaders, those who remain personally committed to uplift me. Thank you for being my life's dancing partners: Luxa, Carla, Pedro, Evelyne, Ana, João, Filipa, Madalena, and Nora. Without you, this book would not even have been considered.

This book started with my intention to pass along what I know keeps saving my life. However, this book would not have gained form or made sense had it not been for the amazing PYP team: Jenn T. Grace, Bailly Morse, Gail Marlene Schwartz, and Erin Walton. Thank you for your practical guidance, effective feedback, corrections, and continued support. Your caring professionalism and dedication have made this book possible.

Table of Contents

Preface

Dancing all the way

What I love most about dancing is feeling the music move me. Being one with the impermanence of the music reminds me that I am already free, alive, home—and I love it. I am a coach, not a farmer or a dancer, nor am I a writer. But because I coach in an unconventional way, clients have often asked me if I would consider writing about what I offer during my sessions. At first I shrugged it off, but over time I noticed a shift within me and found the courage to start sharing my insights. This book is a great example of how I practice what I preach and move through life. In this book, I share my personal practice of accepting life's invitations to dance and invite you—my readers—to practice this dance as well.

Right before the pandemic in 2020, I softly whispered that I wanted to write a book. It was going to be a different book. However, 2020 was a year full of invitations.

Uncertainty was widespread. I was being called to listen to the music being played and be of service. Clients reached out asking for help in dealing with unprecedented conditions in their lives. As I connected with what I noticed in myself, I recognized that my personal power comes when I can be with what is mine in whatever form it shows up. Life seems to bluntly push me to trust the "music," to notice what happens inside, and to respect my own rhythm. Change happens constantly, but I can only dance as I am. The more I realized how important these practices are, the clearer it became to me. I had to write about them. The music had changed, and I listened. I asked for support and started writing, one word at a time, and many corrections later, here it is.

Dear Reader

Shall we dance?

I am grateful that you have accepted my invitation and picked up this book. Something led you to this moment. Perhaps you are facing a transition in life, some undesirable changes, or perhaps you are juggling too many obligations and are stressed or exhausted. Or maybe you have a health condition, or you are bored and feeling flat. Whatever you are going through, I hope you get some creative insights from this book. I hope to inspire you, and I trust that my ideas and stories will serve you.

If my life has taught me anything, it is that my most difficult moments have also carried the most precious insights into who I am and what I am made of. That is why I have learned to value both and now get curious about the challenges and notice what is possible for me. For this reason, I do not work with motivation first. I will not push you, but I will encourage you to know yourself. Your doubts are valid.

I have them too. And yes, underneath all the perceptions of what it should be, the accumulated beliefs and judgements, there is the energy for which we are longing.

Whatever your reason, I am glad you are choosing me to be your coach and dance companion. Although I wrote this book for you, please make this the gift you give yourself— the gift of time for yourself, the gift of courage to see. Invite yourself to open up just a little and to be curious to play with what is *here*. Be creative and make what I offer relevant for you, where you are now. There is no wrong way, but only the invitation to be closer to yourself, to co-create your dance.

Quote

---

*I salute the light within your eyes where the
whole Universe dwells.
For when you are at that center within you
and I am that place within me,
we shall be one.*

—CRAZY HORSE,
OGLALA SIOUX CHIEF, 1877

Introduction

Take me out of here!

Have you ever been in a place where you had dreamed of being, only to find yourself wanting to get out of there? Do you have a picture-perfect, ideal moment you want to be living? I sure have, and it is probably one of the most recurrent feelings in my life. My lack of awareness of my inner road-map and how I am resisting this moment seem to be the reasons my dance does not flow. There seems to be an imaginary better scene controlling my moves, and this alone is a greater obstacle to my well-being, more than any circumstance. With the following story—my 2004 "bus ride" when I was doing my master's field work in Northern Mozambique—I hope to highlight what I have learned and the major invitations of this practice:

A voice screams inside my head as I try to escape the goat chewing my hair. I am sitting up front in an old pickup truck that is serving as a bus in the middle of nowhere. Everyone and everything are squeezed in a space that should comfortably fit half of what it is carrying. Pressed against people, animals, and tools, I try scooting forward but have no room to move. I am literally sitting on a rusty metal spring. The intense odors are nauseating, and the environment is painful to bear. Although I want to be respectful and grateful for the ride, I am visibly tormented. I do not want to be *Here*. I do not understand the dialect and cannot stop feeling my discomfort and pain as emotional hurt. My fellow passengers laugh. They are obviously laughing at me and my lack of ability to navigate this experience. There is nothing funny about the experience, at least not for me.

Refusing to Dance: My Greatest Problem

In this bus, as in life, my attitude has been this: if this bus is life's invitations to dance, I thank you, but my answer is NO. First, I lacked awareness of my own internal system, which prevented me from separating physical pain from emotional pain.[1] I could not identify that the physical pain I was experiencing was being interpreted by my autonomic nervous system as a threat. This interpretation kept me looking for solutions that would not address my needs. Lack of self-awareness can turn a single bus ride into an anxiety trip.

Second, I had the tendency to turn to things that were outside of my control, focusing on what was "wrong." For example, I asked "Why did the vehicle I was traveling in before have to break? Why is this happening to me?" Or, my mind went into the future, asking "When will I get there?" The mind wanted to fix the unfixable and control the uncontrollable. I used to believe that I could relax and enjoy the ride by fixing the physical problem. The rationale was that, once I solved all problems, then I would be okay, but this kept me in a never-ending "doing" mode. Turning to the outer world could solve my physical pain in the bus, but it would not have addressed my emotional suffering.

Third, my mind created solutions that never addressed the real cause of my suffering (because of reasons one and two). I was creating suffering that was worse than the physical pain, and I suffered more because of my imaginary situations, such as wondering if I should be riding in a better bus. Because I was unaware of what was real for me in that moment, I could not see that the cause of my physical pain was the rusty seat. My emotional discomfort, on the other hand, was created by my thoughts and emotions. Had I been able to be in my body and notice my emotions and thoughts, I would not have taken so long to arrive. It was as if I was amplifying—zooming in on the unfamiliar—what was wrong and what was missing. This prevented me from remembering my own intentions, my purpose.

In my confusion, I could not see how supported I was in that moment. Once I changed my focus, I could laugh and regain awareness. I became more present, and I started to remember that I had the ability to rewrite the story and create a different reality for myself, even if physically nothing had changed. According to the Pareto principle,[2] also known by the 80/20 rule, 80 percent of our results are generated by 20 percent of our activity. By focusing on my physical pain and discomfort, and by not being aware of how my brain was creating escape scenarios to regulate my discomfort, I had created the majority of my suffering/problems (the 80 percent). In fact, only 20 percent of my suffering was based on the actual pain of my rusty, unpadded seat. The rest of my suffering was being created inside of me and my own nervous system. **Therefore, my refusal to participate, which is my greatest problem, derives from lack of self-awareness.**

I use the above bus ride as a roadmap for how I create my own reality. First, there is an event that does not go according to plan. In my case, the vehicle I was traveling in broke. Then, the available solution was riding on this "sort of bus." The actual physical circumstances—being squeezed, the goat chewing my hair, the smell of dung, the pain on my bum— were real but did not create my reality. *I* did. I created a reality of suffering with the questions in my mind, the images of what it should be: a better bus, more space, a padded seat, a respectful goat. I was not present in the moment. I was not aware of my own mind in a loop. I was ignorant of the war I was creating inside of me. Thus, my nervous system was creating imaginary solutions. I was imagining alternative scenarios when there was nothing else. I noticed several obstacles in my way, and I was fighting the facts of the present situation, of the bus. Behaving the way I did, I also sold my truth. No wonder I get addicted to anything that promises to take me away from my suffering. This bus ride was a short-lived problem, although I did not see it as such at the time. The fact is that I repeat the same pattern in most areas of my life, and now I know I am not alone in doing so. My ignorance of how I create my reality is worse than any event that disrupts my plan. Unless I notice what is causing what, I will continue wanting to get rid of the discomfort and get into mind loops of alternative realities. This pattern creates more suffering than pain itself.

How many people do you know live in the loop of "this shouldn't have happened" and cause themselves unnecessary stress? There is normally something that disrupts the initial plan. Sometimes all it takes is a little traffic or another driver's forgetting to signal. Other times they go on and on over an incompetent boss or the tinder date who revealed him or herself to be different from their profile. Something disturbs the imagined, often idealized, and emotional discomfort happens. The mind fights the facts and starts presenting images of what it should be. **Unaware of the inner fight and the role we play in creating the struggle, we get stuck.** I am referring to this inner fight—the being stuck in an old loop habit, which prevents us from being present and seeing everything that is really happening—as refusing to be part of the dance.

We tend to follow the same pattern in ourselves and with others. It feels like a vicious cycle. When we are not aware, we continue to turn to what fuels the problem, which interferes with our ability to accurately assess our circumstances. In those moments, we cannot see what is healthy, useful, or beneficial for us. We cannot notice the strategies available to us or find solutions that reflect how we want to respond in the moment. This is precisely what I did on the bus. I resisted the moment and was unable to connect with those around me, to engage, or respond the way I wanted to. My unconsciously learned roadmap was creating a reality of unnecessary suffering.

It is important to acknowledge that the way we learn to create our problems is not entirely our fault. As humans, we are both individual and collective beings. We inherit and get caught in a sort of a collective pattern that carries urban myths; we are sold ideals and images of success and perfection. Our ideals of the promised happiness or a blissful pain-free life end up dictating the template, "Life should be like that...BUT not like this...." No wonder we waste our energy searching for this ideal "something else, never *here*."

We continue to chase the high, hoping to find the utopian "constant happiness." Do you have an ideal postcard, a roadmap for how your life should be?

From personal experience, I know that once I get into the chasing trance, the experience of this moment becomes wrong, unfair, and even a threat. By natural design, the nervous system reacts to what is in the moment. In the bus, I wanted to transform my experience. As I chased the idealized perfect moment, I was avoiding feeling the emotional discomfort of the reality that this moment was not ideal. Sometimes we freeze or just give up and play dead. **We are exhausted and walk around as emotionally depleted bodies;** we carry constant battles inside ourselves. This inner war is emotionally draining, and since our survival nature is designed to avoid pain, we get back into the chase creating a repetitive loop. No wonder we forget our true essence as we "prostitute" ourselves to meet our needs by avoiding pain and seeking pleasure. Nothing outside ourselves can change our roadmap, we become addicted while trying to fix this moment. We search for "the promised better," the high, anything but *this*. We experience "*here*" as a problem that needs to be fixed.

Accepting Life's Invitations

Life was inviting me to join in, to notice, to feel, to connect with, to enjoy. There was nothing to be solved in that bus. "The mystery of life is not a problem to be solved but a reality to be experienced" Van Der Leeuw[3] first said. I can fix a car, but I cannot fix life. I have choices though. In the above story, I could have stepped out of the bus and walked to my destination. This would have solved the goat chewing my hair, feeling the pain on my bum, being squeezed, and feeling nauseated by the odors. However, this would not have solved my inner roadmap, the real cause of my suffering. If I followed this roadmap, nothing would ever fit, even if I thought it did for a moment. What is the solution then?

The solution is to be fully present, having an awareness rooted in my body noticing the many experiences inside myself. An embodied self-awareness allows for distinctions within and allows viewing life, even when uncomfortable, as a flow of experiences—a dance, rather than a problem to be fixed. This is the invitation that life is constantly asking us to accept. Increasing embodied self-awareness allows us to recognize our inabilities. Even though we cannot see our templates, we can know that we have them and that they are working. It is being with the experience that reduces our inner and outer conflicts, restores our ability to assess situations and ourselves, and supports our decision making. Once we accept this moment, we can align the information we receive with our intentions and values as well as our possibilities. This deeper connection within and with others is a life-long practice. In the above example of my bus ride, this happened by chance when I remembered why I had asked to experience something real while I lived in this remote area in Northern Mozambique. Now, I turned this "dance" lesson into a practice.

Accepting and turning our attention to the inner world is not a task to be accomplished, but a habit to be developed. Just like learning a foreign language, it takes practice to become fluent in the many languages of the body, heart, mind, and soul. The process is a reconnecting to nature and to the natural flow of our own systems. It is in remembering who we are that allows the dance and everything that is supporting us in this dance. The floor is underneath us, even when we fall. This is life's invitation to dance from *Here*, and it is possible.

Same Bus Ride, Different Dance

As I look at the woman sitting next to me, hiding her laughter with her hand, I cannot help but smile with her. In this moment, I connect with her. I understand her. I feel her amusement. Still, I hear the voices in my head asking why… "Why me? Why have I paid for this?" As I turn toward my inner battle, fighting and resisting what is, I get curious. The images start showing up. I remember the months I spent planning and wishing for this trip. Wait, what? NO! I did not ask for pain. This was not part of my dream. My memories start answering my questions. My plan was to see, feel, experience, to know what life is like around here. I remembered! I am here, in this bus. We are the lucky ones, the ones who can afford to ride a bus. This is a luxury the majority in this part of the country cannot afford. When I recognize what is happening, I start to notice the many ways I am supported. I notice how precious life is. I relax and smile. The goat does not stop chewing my hair, the odors do not change (or maybe I get used to them). I still do not understand the language. Nothing has changed, but I am now able to experience this moment, pain and all, and enjoy the rest of my journey. Amused by my own fighting and my circumstances, I was no longer refusing to dance. All I needed was to remember. All I had to do was be in the moment. Is your postcard, your ideal perfect moment, preventing you from experiencing what you have been asking for?

Possible Dance Steps

Although there is a sequence to this book, I do not believe that life is a journey. Life is not linear, and there is no logical sequence to the steps you should take. Allow yourself to read this book as it speaks to you. Make it relevant for where you are on your journey. There is only the invitation for you to rest closer to yourself. The stories I share are from my direct experience. When I reference clients, I have changed some identifiable facts to protect their identity and privacy. I use *here* in italics for emphasis. I also use *Selfprint* to refer to the uniqueness of our being. Just like a fingerprint, we all have something unique to us. Each chapter has questions or exercises that I call *Homeplay*, something I encourage you to explore, have fun playing with, and see what you discover for yourself. Start at the end if you feel called to do so. Notice what speaks to you first and follow that.

Chapter 1, "An Unchoreographed Dance," includes an introduction of myself in a way to reveal my shortcomings as well as share what I have learned. I include how I expected a linear ideal journey but life had other plans for me. I learned to dance.

Chapter 2, "Life's Invitations," captures how sometimes it is difficult to learn something new. Most goal-oriented people are following a sort of urban myth of what life should be. There is a belief that life would have more value if it looked a certain way. Learning to accept life's invitations to dance is a process.

Chapter 3, "Four Principles to Fully Dance," communicates the basic coaching principles that guide my practice; I just turn them a little upside down and outside in. They are pointers that facilitate awareness and include the following: 1) we create our realities, 2) what we focus on expands, 3) responsibility is being *here* and seeing our ability to respond, 4) action—let's take the smallest step possible.

Chapter 4, "Obstacles of the Dance," shows us that the obstacles of our dance are not on the dance floor but within ourselves—the fighting, selling ourselves out, the addictions, the being stuck in old broken records. These are what keep us repeating old patterns while expecting different results.

I do not want to have regrets in life and so Chapter 5, "The Last Dance," invites you to connect with your *Selfprint* to know your own rhythm in your dance. I use an imaginary exercise for this—the Deathbed Exercise—which is designed for clarity. I will not ask you to do something I have not done myself, and in this chapter I share my personal experience from my hospital "deathbed."

Chapter 6, "Turning Into Your Inner Music," and chapter 7, "Rewrite Your Moves," offer you suggestions to turn to and connect with your inner power and notice your dance change. I share the importance of asking questions and of questioning what you think you know. As you play with this in your life, notice how you are rewriting your own dance into awareness.

Chapter 8, "Dance Practice," encourages you to begin, to come back to this moment. If you want to start with the practice, start *here* with the eight practices that form the basis for this work. These are my practices. Use them as suggestions, play with them, and find your own. Acceptance requires you to recognize that the music is playing. Turn to yourself and notice what and where the music is touching. Move in three languages: sensations, emotions, and mind. Zoom in and zoom out to come closer and to step back and gain perspective. Let it flow as you remember and reconnect with past and future possibilities. Surrender as you realize you are supported. There is nothing to worry about. Come back *here* again and again. Repetition is the essence of dancing. Be creative and dance your *Selfprint*.

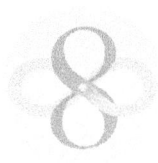

1

An Unchoreographed Dance

Today may not be the day for answers,
but to finally let your heart break open
to the vastness of the question.

—Matt Licata

Have you ever felt that your life is not going according to plan? Like many of my clients, I had a plan, a detailed image of what I needed in life. What I had learned helped me get by in school, be productive at work, and achieve. However, I mistakenly internalized that I could control everything in life. It took me a long time to realize that I can design and rehearse as much as I want, but I cannot choreograph life. Life kept showing me that. Every time I memorized a step, the music would change, just as nature and life change. I have experienced change in more ways than I can possibly count. I know loss, insecurity, and death. This was not the journey I had expected. I am sharing my life experience not as an example, but as one version of what is possible and to show how life has been inviting me to dance.

Growing Up: Not the Ballet I Expected

I was born on a coffee plantation in Angola, then a Portuguese colony in Africa. I lived an uneventful life until I was six years old. Then my 20-year-old cousin died in a car accident, which made me question what it meant to be alive. Then the war for independence began. We moved to Portugal, my father died, and my mother fell into a deep, grieving depression. We kept moving from place to place, surviving only because of the many charitable acts of family, friends, and strangers. I learned to fight for survival, and I proudly fight with perfection to this day.

By the time I turned ten, I had lost many meaningful people in my life including my father, three of my grandparents, and two cousins, along with other relatives. If I zoom in on the difficulties I experienced, I see loss and a miserable life. However, nothing is one-sided, and not everything in my life was difficult or painful. If I zoom out, I also see our extended families stepping in to support us. My maternal grandmother and my aunt came to live with us. My uncles were always attentive and did what they could to support us. We lived in a small village and strangers would drop food by our door. Life kept smiling on us each day in so many ways. Still, this was not the life choreography I wanted. I felt robbed by life.

I felt wrong, different, and not enough. Every cell in my body screamed that I had to fight, to change things, to make me better, to be somewhere else. This is not how it was supposed to be.

Forcing Moves to the "Wrong" Music

Only today can I look back and see that life never failed me. I always found kind, supportive people everywhere—even during a war and being uprooted from a home, a community, and a country, even with loss and death. In every difficulty, I found guidance and opportunities. I had a teacher, Evelyne Bozonet, who saw something in me and encouraged me to continue my studies. I was the first one in my family to earn a bachelor's degree in early childhood education, finishing with the highest grade of that year. An idealist at heart, I wanted to contribute to a better world. At 23, I fell in love with a fellow idealist, a man with a kind heart and a brilliant mind, and I moved to the UK to live with him. I lived in a foreign country and culture, but I carried the same roadmap. This makes me smile now, but back then I cried. All I saw were obstacles: a language I did not master, a culture with unfamiliar norms, and challenging weather. I detest humidity and rain and having an average of 48 inches and 177 rainy days a year was incredibly difficult for me. Everything seemed to be off the ideal choreography.

For a while, I had four part-time jobs at the same time, and I still signed up to study Psychology. I desperately missed my family and friends. I was exhausted, depressed, and angry with myself and with everyone. I was trying so hard, but nothing seemed to work. I used to look at the most amazing green

3

fields, in awe at their beauty, while wondering how I could feel so bad with such beauty outside. I blamed myself and everyone for my unhappiness. Instead of turning to myself and feeling it all, I wanted out. I continued fighting, forcing my choreographed steps to fit. I believed that, if I focused on what I could control, I could fix the "problem."

Starting to Listen Inwards

In 1999, my husband got a job offer and we moved to Santa Fe, New Mexico, USA. The music changed again. I returned to study English and Psychology while volunteering at a school. This program helped integrate children into the school system. The children and their families taught me a great deal about discrimination, privilege, determination, and love. I was forced to learn that obstacles are just information. By seeing others fully, including their circumstances and obstacles, I started to accept the music that life plays. I also learned that, even when we speak the same language, we often cannot understand each other. We understand the words, but because we do not know how our own system works, we cannot identify our emotional needs and often get lost in intentions. Because of my many moves, different languages, and cultures, I believed that culture was the main reason for human communication misunderstandings. At Virginia Tech (VT), I began listening to the music playing, and I saw my inner calling written as my Alma Mater, *Ut Prosim*, meaning "That I May Serve." I changed my major and earned my second degree in communication, focusing on multicultural communication. I wanted to achieve, but life kept inviting me to listen, to be present and enjoy the present experience.

I was told that success goes where energy flows, so I focused and achieved my goal. I was on the Dean's List every year and finished the degree *magna cum laude*. Although achieving my goal felt good, true success was finding intrapersonal communication and starting to turn to my inner world. This relationship with myself opened a new dimension. Life was softly showing me the way.

Starting to Learn to Accept Life's Invitations

Volunteering has been one of the most enriching experiences in my life. It has been an unexpected gift. I used to believe I had something to give but realized that I was the one who received when I volunteered. I have learned more about myself and the world while volunteering than I learned from any structured educational program. I volunteered for VT Women's Center and became involved in violence against women issues. Throughout my seven years as a volunteer and staff member, I doubted that I knew much about violence against women because, until then, I had not been raped, beaten, or abused by a man. Through the complexity of the work, I learned about the pervasive cycle of abuse. Even though we could physically help each individual, we had a greater challenge at hand and that was to recognize and denounce the embedded tolerance of our violent culture.

Through self-work and training, I later learned the problem cannot be solved at the individual level. I had work to do. First, I had to see the violence inherent in myself so I could understand the patterns it took in my behavior and passive tolerance of larger scale violence. I needed to get to know the abusive thoughts and beliefs inside my head if I was to be brave and accept that what was happening to me was abuse. Until I did this, I became stuck in excusing the behavior of the others. For example, during my volunteer work, I often heard "He called me names, but he didn't mean it." Change must start from its roots, but I only have access to my internal individual system. Once I started to see how I participated in the violence, I refused to contribute to the widespread systemic problem. Each event, each connection, seemed to be life telling me to turn inwards and take responsibility for my own life. Once I learned that I had the power to change the relationship with my own inherited abuses and traumas, my life started to change. My ability to accept the current moment and be curious about my own unconsciousness may not seem like much of an achievement, but for me it was and still is. Knowing and seeing are only one step. It is *here* that the dance happens.

My search for answers and thirst to make a difference led me to continue my studies. In graduate school, almost in my 40s, I earned a master's degree in public and international affairs. I thought I had achieved it all. I worked as a research assistant for the Women in International Development office where my main role was to gather data to facilitate gender integration in multidisciplinary projects. The work was meaningful on many levels, and I had a full-time job with a good salary. I also had a meaningful, supportive community. I share this information not to impress you, but to let you know that I achieved goals. I got there, only to be reminded that the dance is ever-changing.

My husband had an irrefutable job offer, and we decided to accept and move to England. While looking for a job, I earned my life coaching certification. Although goals[4] are important in life, these were not my real life's goals. *Here* is life's much bigger invitation. During the coaching training, I continued to seek results. I never wanted to dive deep into the self-work that was required of me. At first, I never intended to work as a coach. I just wanted to know the strategies and have the tools to continue working with capacity building in international development. I never wanted my own business. However, I fell in love with learning about myself and jumped into this new universe of self-discovery. My coaching sessions continued to be pro-bono since I saw them as practice for when I would get back to work with Women in International Development. In fact, I only registered my business when a client refused to accept sessions for free and paid me.

An Unconventional Coach

In 2008, I struggled to come up with a name for my business. I respected life's impermanent nature. I also knew the nature of the work would change. The only constant in life is energy, which changes in form but remains energy. "Upanji" means "energy" in Kimbundu, which is one of the many languages in the country in which I was born. It is also the language of my ancestors. I wanted the wisdom of my illiterate black grandmother and the connections of my peoples' history to be a part of what I was creating. I wanted a name that represented integration of the lessons learned from past experiences while acknowledging the power of the present moment. "Upanji" seemed to fit because it honored that the past and future are *here*. Contrary to anything I expected, my coaching practice grew slowly and organically, flowing with many changes.

In 2013, my husband and I moved to Connecticut in the middle of an extremely cold winter. My body's wisdom used the freezing temperatures to call for my attention. During a session with Matt Licata—my therapist who uses contemplative and mindfulness-based approaches for transformation and healing—he suggested I try Chi-kung. The healing benefits of Chi-kung are millennial, and I enrolled in a class the next day. As I practiced, I noticed what is *here* and surrendered. I let go of the outcome and allowed my body to integrate. *Here*, the moment I practice, I forget the desirable end result and have fun with the mystery of what I cannot see and what is alive in me. It is the dance between the paradoxes of nothing and everything. Needless to say, I fell in love with the practice. The steps have always been *here*. I just could not see them. I was always too busy fighting and hurting. More than any other meditative practice, Chi-kung taught me to consciously slow down and notice my own energy flow. It literally showed me the importance of the dance.

One Tuesday morning in Master Ming Wu's class, my eyes were closed, my hands facing each other, my feet standing wide; I was sensing and "following the chi." I was not intentionally moving right or left, and the movement designed a sphere between my hands. In this sphere appeared the shape of an infinity[5] sign intertwining with the number eight. It was as though the flow of the movement was coming together to show me this energy moving in harmony. This slow dance was happening between my hands, but I could also feel it inside my body. For the first time, I noticed how my inner experience is indeed somatic. Every cell in my body was vibrating in unison, flowing according to what was happening between my hands. My mind was not sure if my inner experience was creating my outer experience or vice versa, but whatever it was, I was loving the flow.

Everything is Already *Here* as Energy

Have you ever been looking for something you thought was missing, only to realize it had been *here* all along? I left class with the image of the infinity sign and the eight in my mind. I shared my experience during a session with Joana, a client who happened to be an architect. The image aligned perfectly with the work we had been doing together. Joana had wanted to change her life's direction and was fighting the outside world, her work, and the social expectations she faced. Her struggle could be seen in the sphere. The intertwining flow of the lower part of the eight appeared heavy but constant. This was part of Joana's problem as she allowed her past and others to drag her down. The top part of the eight became lighter, more fluid, with possibilities for her future. The sphere contains the physical body, in the eight figure, which is heavy and strong. The flow helped Joana "see" her future and the lightness in herself. In the present moment, she had the choice whether to dance or not. Joana had danced all her life, and as a child she had wanted to be a ballerina. She stepped into the flow immediately.

Joana saw that if she narrowed her focus and zoomed in on the problem, she felt bad and lost. If she zoomed out, she could see what was possible in the future. This knowledge made Joana feel sad because she knew what was missing and was fearful of the changes required for her to feel differently. It can be overwhelming to see it all at once. Therefore, the invitation is to come back to the present moment and zoom in just enough to get information and zoom out a bit so as to not be swollen up by what is arising in us. This zooming in and zooming out opens one possibility at a time. Joana could see she had room for this dance, this first step, just one step at a time. She started with her physical space and did a major cleanup. First she changed her living space by making small choices regarding what would and would not stay in her life. She shared the photo of the shelf she had repainted with a light color. The caption said, "Fresh paint, feeling much lighter now."

Joana saw herself as this energy, her struggles, her resistance to be herself for "the good of others," and she saw herself as this infinite energy just by being alive. Joana took one step then. She also designed the image, the sphere as wholeness with the eight and the infinity. Upanji's logo gained a tangible form that day. With the logo came the realization of how connected the symbol was to my own unchoreographed dance.

Dancing All Along

Today, it is easy to see that it was not the degrees or certificates, but life itself that was training me all along. It was as if life had given me the opportunity to gather a diverse set of tools for my new role as a life coach, along with any experience I might need. On the outside, it has been helpful to learn information and practical tools, but on the inside, it has been more important to slow down, give space, and be aware of each moment. The outside only confirms the inner experience. By falling in love with the present moment,[6] we find what we have been looking for all along. Although I knew this in my heart, my belief was reiterated by author and teacher Jeff Foster. While reading his book called, *Falling in Love with Where You Are*, I realized everything is always already *here*. I only notice when I have the awareness inside, as if it is this inner knowing that allows the experience to gain visible form. In presence and authenticity, we touch wholeness. The dance has been happening all along. Before, I judged my life as wrong and so I wanted to fix it. **Now I see that what I saw as a problem to be solved was a melody to which I could dance.** I am grateful to have failed at choreographing my life so I could accept life's invitations to dance. Do you have an ideal choreography for your life?

8   ○   ∞

Homeplay

I call it *Homeplay* for a reason: when we play, there are no right ways or wrong ways to play. Explore, feel, touch, taste, smell, experience. If you feel drawn to turn into yourself, here are a few suggestions. Have fun with these ideas or explore others that might call out to you. If you want to go deeper into this practice visit www.upanji.com.

1. If you were to create a timeline of your life, what events would you include? What would you exclude? What was your criteria?
2. How do you feel when you look at your timeline? What if you created another one with a different title?

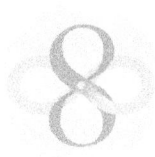

2

Life's Invitations

*The only way to make sense out
of change is to plunge into it,
move with it and join the dance.*

—ALAN WATTS

Learning to Accept Life's Invitations to Dance

Do you tend to accept invitations or hang on to previous plans? Being too controlling,[7] I took a long time to accept that my plan would not always develop according to my wishes. In retrospect, as it is always easier to see when we look back, I held on too tightly to my childish mental imagery of life. When I finally let go and stopped resisting what was, I gained more than I could possibly have predicted. These invitations to dance are not always easy to accept, but in my experience, they are much more rewarding. It takes practice: first to notice that the music playing has changed, then to notice our ability to move accordingly. **What matters is that we give ourselves permission to explore and see what is possible.** Both Julia's and Kathy's stories show that regardless of how the dance will end, all we need is to take the first step.

Julia first wanted some help with her relationship. She missed the connection she had with her husband when they were first dating. Now they were parents of a three years old, and Julia felt her partner was not the same anymore. At first, she blamed herself and excused his behavior because of cultural differences and his past relationships. During the first few sessions, Julia wanted strategies to communicate better and feel connected again. While applying some strategies we discussed, Julia opened up more in our work together. Occasionally, she would drop bits of important information. For example, she shared that her husband was extremely jealous and controlled her use of both her phone and schedule. He had lost his temper a few times. As a result, Julia grew more silent at home and became fearful that he could hurt her.

There is a vital distinction between accepting life's invitations and tolerating abuse. In Julia's case, it was crucial to call things by their names, mainly recognizing his behavior was abusive. Acknowledging abuse provided information to determine the next course of action. Without acceptance of what is, we continue to make excuses and become misguided. Accepting what is can be as simple as saying it is raining when it is. Refusing to recognize rain denies me the possibility of choosing accordingly. Without acceptance that it is raining outside, I deny myself the opportunity to choose the appropriate clothing or choose to not go out at all. **Acceptance is connecting what is true and real with how I experience and feel about the circumstances.** I often do not know how to accept, and I know I am not alone. We have been indoctrinated by many ideas of how something should be that we do not recognize what is real in this moment. Our families and communities of origin help us acquire and adjust to social norms. I was taught to be agreeable and quiet, as good girls should be. Practicing acceptance shows me that my experience in a situation is not always agreeable. When this happens, being pleasant may not be an option and nothing inside me is quiet.

Trapped in so many concepts and dreams, Julia could not see what was happening with her. As we talked about her goals and what she wanted to create, Julia revealed her day-to-day as well as her imaginary dream life. She came from a religious family that valued the sanctity of marriage, and she prioritized keeping the family together. Ever since she was a child, Julia had dreamed of having a supportive marriage. When she and her husband first started dating, they talked about the life they wanted to create together. In our sessions, Julia had serious difficulties reconciling her expectations— the ideals of marriage—with reality. Every time Julia got closer to recognizing how she felt, she refused to accept that what she was telling me was her life. She kept facing the obstacle of acceptance.

Our work together involved aligning these two apparent opposites. Julia became capable of turning into herself and becoming aware of her inner world. She started to identify thoughts and feelings she had never noticed before. Gradually, Julia no longer wasted her energy trying to change her husband. Instead, she focused on taking care of her inner ability to respond to her situation. When challenges emerged, she learned to notice what was possible for her. When her husband grabbed her phone to read her messages, Julia started noticing what was happening within herself. She felt a sense of injustice. Her mind raced with the idea that she had to stop him. She feared conflict and dreaded images of her daughter growing up in a screaming environment along with future scenes of abuse. The situation before us is our invitation to become more aware of our own systems. When we become aware that what runs us is mostly unconscious, we are not setting ourselves up to change it. Quite the contrary; we are given the opportunity to recognize the unconscious and unspoken stories that are constantly running in the background. Slowly, Julia became clear about the environment she wanted to raise her daughter in. She wanted music playing, laughter, conversations, and shared household chores. She wanted her daughter to learn from her what it is to be a woman and be respected in a relationship with others.

The more Julia realized how her own dreams and ideals were creating her frustration, the closer she saw the truth of her experience. No excuses, just noticing. She felt sad, but less fearful. There was no possible script. She had to listen to the music playing outside herself, as well as inside. **Acceptance requires willingness to not have a predetermined answer, a ready move.** Acceptance takes practice. For Julia, it took practice to read the environment and her husband's moods, while noticing her own thoughts, emotions, and body reactions. Dancing requires trusting that life has our best interests in mind. It is true that we are biologically designed for survival. Our nervous system is wired to support us, which it does by sending messages and signals. The challenge is to hear the music and enter a space where we can hear both inside and outside cues. In this space, there is no one leading and no one following; there is one body listening, feeling the music, and being moved by the sounds. When we fall in love with this music and are in this space, nothing else exists and everything is *here* already. We become our body, becoming one with the movement, the music, and the space itself. Only life can do this, and once we touch life, we become leaders. How in love with life are you?

Learning to accept the unacceptable is not always easy when we are emotionally invested. The images we have created in our mind prevent us from seeing the whole truth. One of my first interests in studying Psychology was our human tendency for confirmation bias. British psychologist Peter Wason first introduced the hypothesis with the triples of number rule experiment in the 1960s. He reasoned we tend to look and recall what confirms our beliefs. According to psychologist and economist Nobel Prize winner Daniel Kahneman,[8] in an interview with Baer[9] said, "Confirmation bias comes from when you have an interpretation, and you adopt it, and then, top down, you force everything to fit that interpretation. That's a process that we know occurs in perception that resolves ambiguity, and it's highly plausible that a similar process occurs in thinking." Biases are engrained in human logic errors. We stop receiving information that contradicts our beliefs. To stop questioning is dangerous because we become complacent, victims of an outdated image that no longer serves us. Again, abuse is never acceptable. **What we accept is the fact that it is happening.** What we do with the information is for us to decide. Just like on the dance floor, we have the freedom to choose how to move. Sometimes we learn to accept that we do not like the music we hear.

Imagine you are on the dance floor and love the song you hear. You are dancing your heart out, but the music comes to an end and the next song starts to play. You continue on the dance floor until you feel that your heart is not in it. You lose your flow, and there is something you cannot quite name. Then you realize you simply do not like the song that is playing. When the music changes, what do you do? Do you continue dancing on the dance floor but not as engaged? Do you just keep kind of dancing in place? Do you go ask the DJ to change the song? Do you take this opportunity to get something to drink, go to the restroom? What do you do when the music changes?

One day, Julia came beaming into a session. Her smile was larger than her face could hold. Julia had started to respect herself and had decided to ask for a divorce. She was well aware of the difficulties ahead, and her face closed up when she started listing all she had to change in her life. Her eyes, however, brightened again when she talked about her religious values, the guiding principles of her life, and the mother she wanted to be. Julia was choosing to live true to herself. She shared what was most important for her: love, respect, support, and contribution. She wanted her daughter to learn that being strong is not yelling or threatening others, that everyone deserves respect, and that she always has a choice. The more Julia talked about her daughter, the stronger she became. Julia wanted to share her detailed plan with me while asking for my support because she knew it would be difficult. I congratulated Julia for her courage to be aware, for her willingness to take practical steps, and for the self-care she was showing in learning to accept life's invitations to dance. Her situation was real, and she was learning how to dance to the music being played in her life.

Saying yes to life's invitations to dance is both learning to recognize the music playing as well as what is ours. There is always a world of outside circumstances and tons of information I do not control. At the same time, humans have a vast amount of internal information happening. There are former experiences, judgements, sensations, emotions, feelings, thoughts, and expectations. Everything is happening at the same time and accepting is simply recognizing what is what and being with it all. Just like when we hear music, we cannot control what we hear, but we can notice specifically the drums, the guitar, or other instruments. Life is all of it, not just what we like. **Life does not give us a sound box with controls.** We cannot adjust or eliminate the offensive sounds to our ears, but we can recognize what is uncomfortable to our system at this time.

Kathy, a Psychology graduate who was looking for a job, came to me for help with practical interviewing strategies. She knew the theories much better than I did. What Kathy needed was some practical guidance in accepting the music playing. She was looking for a job in the corporate world, but her personality and dressing style did not match the requirements. As a soft-spoken introvert, who blushed when asked to speak up, she found the interviewing process challenging. The dress code, the formal setting, and her being center stage were not her tunes to dance to. We started by distinguishing how she felt when at her best. Kathy described she could be comfortable, even chatty, when discussing a topic that interested her. I asked her what emotion gave her that sensation of chattiness. Her answer was "passion." We played with the word passion and how that made her feel in her body. While identifying what passion felt like for her and what could give her that reminder of passion during her interview,

Kathy blushed as she said, "an animal print lingerie." We laughed and joked with the idea and she decided to give it a try. First, she imagined herself interviewing in a required corporate business apparel while wearing a leopard skin print underwear.

The smaller the first step, the easier it is to notice little shifts inside. Kathy noticed her amusement and her passionate personality being present. She noticed the contrast: feeling safe and feeling the judgements of what she believed an animal print lingerie would suggest about her. She accepted that all this was present, as was her fear of failing the interview process. Kathy envisioned the interview process and continued to notice the people interviewing her were only people playing their roles. Imagining the process started to relax her too. Accepting it all gave Kathy room to feel more comfortable with her own difficulties. She was not trying to change who she was but was becoming aware of what was there. By noticing her circumstances, she could choose healthy, useful, and beneficial ways to respond. The interview happened, and Kathy confessed she did not have the courage to buy animal print lingerie. However, she did wear sexy underwear as a reminder to feel passionate about herself, the areas of work that interested her, her vision, and what she has to offer. When we spoke after the interview, Kathy had not heard back from the company. She said that at some level, she was okay if she did not get the job because she felt good about her answers. Kathy is now more comfortable noticing the images showing up in her head and welcoming them, as well as feeling passionate in her body. This is acceptance. Kathy did end up getting the job. If only we did not grow up with images of what we ought to be.

The Imaginary Dance

*If the path before you is clear,
you're probably on someone else's.*

—JOSEPH CAMPBELL

Have you ever been asked what you want to be when you grow up? Not all children want to grow up, but many dream of adult life. Regardless of which group we fall into, the reasons for wanting to grow up or wanting to stay children are the same. Autonomy, freedom of choice, independence, and being different can be both attractive as well fearful for children. Although those asking the question might be referring to a job or a career, unwillingly, children start learning that maybe they should know how they want their lives to look when they are adults. What children imagine is mainly related to their environment or an outside influence such as a story they heard or personalities they admire.

We start imagining life as adults, then later the school system reinforces the idea we should know where we are heading. Somewhere along the way we start believing we must determine the results in our lives. We study and get good grades—or not. Either way, we learn we can control results because we got the gold stars, or we did not get good results and feel bad for failing. Even though I could influence some results like the grades earned, I could not and cannot determine or control life. However, there is a sense we should control where we are and what we have. We extrapolate this learning to wanting to control *this dance.* Joseph Campbell shares, "If you can see your path laid out in front of you step by step, you know it's not your path. Your own path you make with every step you take. That's why it's your path." Do you believe you should have your path laid out in front of you? Is this your childhood vision? Check again. Sometimes we plan and want to keep the plan alive, however, we need to be flexible with room for growth.

There is a place for plans, goals, and strategies. Even when the goal is to not have a goal, *that* is a goal. I have nothing against plans, quite the opposite. I am a control freak (in recovery). I love to plan, strategize, and organize. What I am referring to is that, while I can plan a trip or organize a party, I cannot plan LIFE! It is impossible. For example, if I plan a trip and buy a flight ticket, my actions are directly connected to outcomes. I pay money and get a ticket. This is a material result. However, in the nonmaterial world of thoughts, sensations, and ways to experience an event, there is no control. With a plane ticket, I cannot control whether I will have a good time. I can only be present with what arises to the best of my ability. Still, we can do our best. Unfortunately, we mistake things, like flight tickets, for the way we experience life and apply the same control strategy for everything, even the things we cannot control. We might go on vacations or own the latest fashion, but we cannot control the end result. Maybe we have loud hotel neighbors or maybe we get food poisoning or get robbed. We have no control over what can happen. Comparatively, there are more circumstances outside of our control than within our control. **Relinquishing control requires a willingness to learn as we go.** Life is not fixed, nor is it linear[10] (at least not the emotional and mental aspects of it).

Do you see life as a journey? What is your destination? Although it is an overused analogy, I do not understand life to be a journey. I once saw a video where Alan Watts said something along the lines of, If life was a journey, no one would want to get to the destination. The first time I heard this, I felt like someone had lived my own experience. Life cannot be about getting there. Instead, it is about life itself—now, with what is—and allowing it all to show up. That is what we are longing for. We have just been misled to look for something else outside of this moment. I believe we are looking for ourselves, this inner knowing that we can trust in our bodies, the music that is playing even when it is not the music we want to hear. *I am here.*

Have you ever known someone who spent his entire life right on track and did everything he was supposed to? Did he find himself questioning his life on his deathbed? If only he had known what he does know now. Would he feel this way about his life? Would he have spent those long hours playing games and sitting in front of the TV? Would he have bought all that stuff? We all know good people who have done this, and most of us have done it too. We followed a predetermined model that we believed to be the only way, and so we did what we thought we were supposed to do. We followed along as if we were riding a nonstop fast train. We followed the script and spent our days checking and sticking to the plan. If this is the calling of our hearts, I have nothing to say. However, I tried, and it was not for me. I refused to follow a preestablished plan, even if the plan was created by my younger self many years ago. I have changed.

Value Moves

You might ask, "If I don't follow a script, if there's no recipe to follow, how do I know I am living life as I am supposed to?" This "supposed to," the postcard, keeps us quite busy looking for ways to get *there*, to the idealized life. What we often forget is that this goal, this ideal dreamed life, (fill in the blank of what that is for you), is the only thing preventing us from living. Life has value just because it is life, not because of what we accomplish. We can (and should) do something. I believe we should add value, we should create. Both are part of our human condition and both are necessary and important. That said, however, it is not what we do that defines the value of our lives. Somehow, we learned that money, titles, and possessions give us value. The more we attribute meaning and value to things and results, the less we can be with what is being lived *here*. The experience of this moment has value for what it is. We already know how to value what is, we do it with nature, and we are also nature.

What have you learned to value? We do not value a tree only when it is giving shadow or fruits. The fruits have value, yet we know the fruits are not the only thing that gives value to a tree. Even though humans are a part of nature, we often forget to extend the same courtesy to ourselves. In my experience, both personally and with clients, I see that when we get going and doing, we often neglect our inherent value. I, too, sometimes forget to feel where the music is and what it is asking of me. I forget to dance. Instead, I turn into a performer, following and copying someone else's choreography. Instead of listening and allowing the move to emerge in its full value, I keep chasing in the trance that this moment is wrong. I worry about failures and mistakes. Sometimes, I do not even know what I am chasing anymore. I forget to value this dance move, maybe because it does not feel safe to not know the full script. Nature is not safe, but maybe safety is not what being alive is about.

The movement that appears in this human body has value. As we notice all sorts of alarms inside—warnings from the mind, its acquired lessons and projected expectations—do we value what is *here*? When I pause and become aware that, in this moment I have a choice, I feel so much more alive. Similar to when I am dancing, I have a choice as I feel the music and let the music move through me. I either allow the move to flow, or I can force my body to move in other ways. In this moment, I learn who I am beyond the obvious of what I had previously internalized I am. In this moment, I can create my experience, my reality. We can do the same, and although there is no single approach that fits everyone all the time, we can play with possibilities. While exploring many strategies and tools, I selected four major coaching principles that help me come back to the moment of possibilities.

8   O   ∞

Homeplay

Do you have space to be *here* with yourself? Play with what resonates with you now.

1. Do you have a childhood memory of how you imagined your life as an adult would look? If you do not have a memory, imagine what your younger self imagined about life as an adult. What comes to mind? Any inherited expectations? Any influences? You can just see it in your mind's eye, or you can write it down, draw or paint what comes up, or you can dance it away.
2. If your life was a dance, what type of dance would it be? Salsa, Kizomba, Ceremonial, Freestyle, Square Dance, Ballet, Forró, Fusion, Interpretive... a combination?
3. Has your "dance style" changed over the years? If yes, did you initiate the change or was it forced upon you?

3

Four Principles to Fully Dance

Nobody cares if you can't dance well.
Just get up and dance.
Great dancers are not great because
of their technique,
they are great because of their passion.

—MARTHA GRAHAM

When the Dance Shakes

Do you tend to resist any change or just the unplanned change? It is said that change is our only constant. Expected change seems to be easier to welcome, but when something happens that I did not ask for or enjoy, I jump into control mode. I turn unpredictable events into problems and dive into action, creating solutions that more often than not fail to address the real issue. This frantic, reactive tendency of finding solutions creates a hamster wheel effect. How can we stop, gain awareness, understand what the real issue is? How can we turn the focus to what really needs attention and create a possible strategy to truly address the facts? The four principles that I share in this chapter are the major guidelines of my work. There are many valuable coaching principles, but these I find to be the most effective in turning myself to what makes a difference. My role as a coach is to invite clients to see beyond the obvious in their deep-rooted perceptions, to own what is real and find their own rhythm. In flow, we see our own uniqueness and how intrinsically connected we are. **Dancing with being *here*, seeing beyond, and zooming in and zooming out is the practice.**

I often use the example of an earthquake. Feel free to replace the word "earthquake" with your specific challenge, problem, or situation. For those of you who have been through an earthquake, please forgive me as I do not speak from personal experience. I purposefully chose a natural occurring disaster that happens from a sudden release of energy, because it is easier to not place blame on external circumstances for its occurrence. When we cannot assign blame to a person, we are more willing to accept facts and see what we cannot change. Even when the situation is intense and life-threatening, the first step is always to see what is present. I usually have an introductory session before anyone chooses to work with me so we can connect. During the session, I explain my work standards and the following four principles:

1. I create my reality, not facts
2. What I focus on expands
3. Responsibility
4. Action

The Earthquake

Earthquakes are real, an undeniable fact of nature. Even so, an earthquake cannot create our reality. The event is the music playing, maybe the same to all, but our dance is different from anyone around us. We dance the way we feel the music, just as people react to events in many ways. We can freeze, panic, stay calm, scream, cry, run away, reach out, or help others. The way a person experiences the earthquake is how they **create reality.**

Our reality is reinforced by what we focus on and this is what will expand. If we focus on how everything got destroyed, we probably feel a certain way that will reinforce itself when we look for how much else is destroyed. However, if we focus on how blessed we are to still be alive, we will feel very differently and will probably look for other ways in which we are blessed. We can use our own confirmation bias to filter the way we read events, or we can become aware of facts as well as our focus. By noticing what is happening in this moment, we expand awareness itself. This also increases our choices. **What you focus on expands.**

In an earthquake, we might think that it is our responsibility to fix the situation or to find a solution. But before we try to rebuild, our **responsibility** is to check in, *here* and now. We must check in with our **ability to respond.** Since abilities are dependent on internal circumstances and on the surrounding environment, it is only in the moment that we can know how we will respond. We cannot predict what emotions will come up, what sensations will be present, or how our surroundings will look. We cannot have a pre-determined ideal of even being helpful, as this might lead us to ignore a wound and hurt ourselves even further. A well-intended desire to be helpful might put others at risk. In the present moment, we take all the information and assess the risk of a collapsing structure and its gravity. When we want to support others, we first must come back to this moment and assess our emotional as well as our physical ability to respond. If we want to contribute effectively to the good of all, we must start *here*. This moment is where possibilities rest, not in the future or alternative moments. Checking-in brings us back to the ability to choose the best possible action.

Action is needed, and as humans we need to act on what is *here*, even in an earthquake. Once we assess our ability to respond, we must determine the best course of action for us at this time. This action cannot be predetermined because we need to check in first and see our situation. Even if the action requires us to stay still for a bit, this is the possible **action for us at the moment.** We learned in school that we must be prepared and have a prompt answer at the tip of our tongues. But in life the answer can only be given in the moment. Some-times the solution will be for what we have prepared for, but not always. Physically, we can be a well-prepared firefighter, but for life, for the Self, we cannot ignore what is *here*. When we act on automatic mode, we might be causing more hurt or damage than if we honor our emotions and our thoughts. Although the concept is simple, it is not so easy to understand because it defies our illusions and our old experiences that we have projected into our lives. This example invites us to see our own obstacles while being present. *Here*, we can own our power to create our own reality.

Principle 1: I Create My Reality

Mike was seeing me unwillingly. He came because his wife had forced him to see me. When I asked him directly, Mike was honest and told me he had a plan: he would just attend sessions for a while to keep his wife happy and then would continue his life as he had always done. I asked Mike how his approach was working for him, and he opened up with me. His wife was very demanding, always wanting more. He felt bad about their arguments, but he loved her and just did his thing when she was not looking. However, the arguments continued. I asked him: if he loved his wife, wouldn't he like to feel closer to her as opposed to hiding and running away from her? Mike said he had given up. I suggested, since he was planning to come to sessions anyway, to just work on himself and the reality he wanted to create. At first Mike did not believe me, but he felt he had nothing to lose.

The disbelief happens frequently when I first introduce the principles to my clients, telling them principle number one is: "You create your reality." I can hear their thoughts when they shake their heads: *If you knew my stories, you would not say such a thing. I did NOT create those!* I see them focusing on the facts about something that had happened that they did not like or want. When we turn only to the facts or the events, we become disconnected from the experience in the body and our thoughts. Of course, we do not create nor do we control other people, facts, or circumstances, no matter how true they are. But we do create our own reality.

For the purpose of this work, I will turn to my inner experience, paying attention to what happens in my belly, legs, and heart in the moment. What sensations, emotions, and thoughts run through my head? Am I creating this reality? My system is active; what I am experiencing inside is my reality. How my inner system is receiving and interpreting this moment is what determines my attitudes and my responses, whether pleasant, unpleasant, resistance, or suffering. I only create how I feel the music, which includes my ability to hear and to translate that into movements and my dance. First, I invited Mike to notice his reality. What was happening with him? What meanings was he giving to each situation? What were his sensations and his thoughts? He knew he would not change his wife, but Mike believed she was the one creating his reality. Assumptions like these misguide our minds as we actively work to change what is often unchangeable, and we do not notice what we are actually creating. The mind is too fast at interpreting situations as problems that need to be solved. From this perspective, we jump to change the facts and the music playing. Most of us did not learn to notice what is inside. We distance ourselves from our own inner experience of this heart racing or this thought, and we turn to the situation outside with the purpose of fixing it. Still, it was when Mike came back to himself that he made the connection. His reactions were to his thoughts and beliefs, not to his wife. What he was living was his reality, but it was not created by his wife or any other factor external to himself. We create things, tools, and art, and even compose music, but these are objects, and they do not create our experience.

My reality is not the event itself, but how I live these circumstances. By refusing to internalize that what happens is a fact (and not his reality), Mike was missing out on what he was creating, even when he could influence some outcomes in a situation. For example, he thought he had a problem because of "the music playing" which were his wife's requests. Even though Mike did not create his wife's demands, he felt that they were his reality. The truth is, his reality was how his inner system was reading, interpreting, and living with his wife's requests. His reality was, consciously or unconsciously, his thoughts about the situation. This included his sensations, his attitudes, his behaviors, his hiding, and his belief that nothing could be done or changed. The facts were there, and although he could not control his wife, he could choose how to deal with her demands. His response was up to him. He could create a different reality.

I asked Mike to state his facts. He had a long list of demands and characteristics about his circumstances and his wife's personality. I asked Mike to turn to himself and only see how he experienced the facts. How did they feel in his body and mind? Mike said that he hides in his office, pretending not to hear her. His body becomes agitated, and he wants her to stop. Mike said he feels like eating and makes plans to go walk the dog. As Mike describes his inner experience, he stops; he understands that this suffering was his reality. His wife was a fact that he could not control. I continued asking Mike questions. If he could change anything, how would he live and experience his situation? How would he want to see and react to the situation? Mike answered promptly that he wanted his wife to change, to be left alone, and to feel appreciated for all he does. I asked, of all those, which depended on him alone? Mike answered, he wants to be patient and respond in the way he knows it is best for them as a couple. Now we were starting to have a sense of what reality Mike wanted to create.

Being unaware of how we are creating our realities is a problem. We may do this unconsciously, but that is what is creating our reality. Noticing the meaning we give to the facts determines how our system can experience them. Our system's capacity depends on the temperament we were born with, past experiences, our emotional and behavioral responses, and the ability with which we integrate the lessons we learned. The important point to highlight is that **our reality is what is happening within ourselves** much more than the outside facts, people, and circumstances.

When I asked Mike what meaning he was giving to his wife's requests, he stopped, thought for a few seconds, and started justifying himself. I asked him to only tell me the meanings he gives to the requests. He answered, "She is impossible to please and is unreasonable." I asked him, "How do you feel when you think that way?" He said she was not always like that. I stopped him and asked how he felt when he thought that way. He responded, "Small, with no voice." He seemed to blush a little while sharing more about his wife and why she did what she did. Gradually, Mike was no longer reducing his wife's character to a behavior and started seeing her in a much more complex, human way. It was as if, by noticing his interpreted meanings, he could see the difference between who his wife was as a human being (complex as this might be) and what she did in specific behaviors. Mike understood his wife's intentions and why she did what she did. He could see what needs she was trying to meet and why. Seeing both the facts and the meanings allowed Mike to identify that how he felt was an old feeling from when his mother would criticize him. Without realizing it, Mike was creating a reality that was not beneficial for him. It was time to consider focus and move to principle number two.

Principle 2: What I Focus on Expands

Have you ever learned an expression and suddenly started hearing it everywhere? I am not referring to trends or new circumstances that generate their own vocabulary, such as "self-isolate" or "ecoanxiety." The first time I heard the expression "empty suit," referring to someone in a leadership role who lacked the necessary skills and competence for the position, I thought the expression was visually amusing. Nevertheless, during that week I heard the same expression another three times. I felt as if once I focused on the creative imagination of the expression, I unknowingly made it relevant. What if we focus consciously in our embodied rich life? **Focus is a skill that we can develop with practice.** Our inner world is hidden and invisible to the naked eye, just like an unknown expression. To make the inner world visible, we must notice the subtle signs already in our body. As we begin to focus, we increase our understanding as well as our physical ability to be present. This awareness gives us a conscious choice, allowing for small distinctions and the possibility of seeing what we can or cannot transform. What we focus on expands[11] because our system receives and transports billions of pieces of information from the external world through our senses and into our brain. It is through the Reticular Activating System (RAS) that enormous amounts of information get filtered and organized. Without it, we would be overloaded with information. The RAS protects us from overwhelm by holding onto, moving, and translating information. Once we understand how the system works, we can use it to our benefit. RAS is simple. When it captures information, it starts working. It does not matter if the information comes from the outside, inside, or does not exist. The process works the same way. The mind/body connection just experiences it fully each time. Whether you imagine your greatest adventure or it is in front of you, your system still gets activated. How often are you afraid when watching a movie? You know it is not real, but once the input enters your system you react as if it is real. You have the same physical sensations, the same emotions, and the same thoughts you would probably have if it was really happening. All this is unconscious.

Learning to Use Our System

The RAS, therefore, needs to know what is important and what is not. Either consciously or unconsciously, we are informing our system of what to prioritize by focusing on something and giving it time, relevance, or intensity. The information gets amplified by what is present and how it will filter what comes next. Hence the saying, what you focus on expands! The first time I thought of the importance of focus was when reading Pam Grout's book *E Squared: Nine Do-It-Yourself Energy Experiments That Prove Your Thoughts Create Your Reality*. As I read the book, I did one of the exercises inviting me to focus on something. I picked yellow cars and I spent the day amazed by how many I was seeing. I saw so many that I started photographing them in case no one would believe me. Perhaps I could not believe it myself.[12]

Have you ever bought a new car and suddenly that is all you see? Many of us have had this experience. Suddenly, we see our car everywhere. The car was already there, but we were just not focusing on it. If our unconscious is so effective already, can we imagine what is possible when we consciously use our focus toward what makes the most difference? When we shift our focus from the unconscious to the conscious, our RAS learns and filters this new focus as important. Please note that I am advocating for consciousness and not positive thinking. If you use affirmations as a positive thinking strategy and it works for you, please continue and ignore what I am about to say. I have done positive thinking practices and affirmations like many, which was a great starting point for my curiosity about this self-discovery dance. Positive thinking can be useful when it is not turned into an either/or. I believe, however, that it is unhealthy to limit ourselves to ONLY thinking positively. The excessive concern, sometimes even fear, of having any other kinds of thoughts is counter-productive, and the tension creates the opposite of the intended effect. The RAS reads intensity as important, something to watch out for, so whatever we try so hard to not focus on gets amplified. This is typically what happens with prohibitions; it turns the focus to what is not allowed, calling our attention to it. Humans are whole; we cannot be cut in half. Conscious focusing means turning our focus into noticing it all, the whole experience, both positive and negative.

After my father's death, I became a pessimist, the kind who would not allow myself to dream for fear of feeling disappointed. The thought "Better safe than sorry" worked for me. My response was understandable since I did not know how to grieve. Instead, I was avoiding painful experiences altogether.

I literally collected daily occurrences that went wrong, and needless to say, what I was focusing on expanded. I was all doom and gloom, and it lasted until I was eighteen when a friend invited me to attend a meditation group. There was something about that place—the people and the practices—that I fell in love with. I was beaming and completely eager to learn and apply the teachings to perfection. Thinking positively and using positive energy was part of cleaning my vibration and rising above my human condition. My prayers had been answered. I would finally overcome limiting myself. It was an amazing time in my life, but I was playing a role, the role of "I am above-human." I worked so hard to avoid any thought that might not be elevated that I was not seeing the whole of me. I had jumped from one extreme to another and all for the same reason: to avoid feeling all those unpleasant human feelings. Our natural design includes emotions, and I was using all my energy to avoid them. Looking back, I admire my reasonable success at both attempts. Running away from what is not pleasant is my specialty. Working with acceptance is decisive for me. Jeff Foster's book, *The Deepest Acceptance*, started to break open some pieces of me. Embracing my whole self has been my practice since. After I reached out to Matt Licata, my therapist and later teacher, my fake personas started to wear off. The hard shell started to break, and as Jeff and Matt say, as I befriended myself, I no longer aimed for extremes. My practice is the recognition of what is *here*. The more I turn to this being that I already am, the more I see. That is why I am inviting you to join me. Are you willing to shift the energy you are wasting on running away and fighting yourself and invest it in living as you are?

This being *here* practice is an embodied self-awareness, a kind inclusion for wholeness. Denying parts of ourselves can be a waste of energy. Still, that is the focus of many transformational techniques. Fighting is an integral part of life (even if we do not like it or it does not feel good), but fighting our most natural features imprisons us in unproductive tasks. Awareness does not dismiss truth. It uses that information to our benefit. Embodied self-awareness gives attention to what is *here* so we can truly learn, grow, and expand consciously. When we live from this place, we become equipped to choose what is for us in each moment. Unless we command our focus, we get distracted easily and fall into our old habits. *Here* is the field of possibilities, but if I am never present, how can I access what is possible? Sometimes I run on automatic mode, which is what my body has learned from past experiences. This is most likely an old habit that might not be suited for this moment or for who I am now. When I see myself as I am, when I can focus on all that is happening inside myself, I can feel the music move me from inside out. I am dancing.

Because of Mike's childhood experiences, he was unconsciously focusing on his trigger: his wife's requests. Even when Mike understood and agreed to what needed doing in the present moment, because of how he had felt as a child (feeling small and with no voice), he just wanted to get out of there. Although this cycle was unconscious in his body, his system reacted to his sensations. Trigger: wife's requests, Focus: Mike's meaning "She is impossible to please and is unreasonable," Reaction: old intense body sensations. The RAS senses the intensity and signals the brain to focus on it and prioritizes it. When Mike's wife asks him to do something in the house or with their son, he feels the request as a possible threat. Mike gets stuck in a loop.

Even though I am not a therapist, what I have studied about trauma indicates that when a reaction to an event is disproportionately intense, it might be because of a traumatic event in the past. There are two main categories of trauma: developmental trauma and shock trauma. Developmental trauma starts in early childhood and happens to children who experience multiple or prolonged adverse events over a period of time. Dr. Bruce Perry, renowned psychiatrist and researcher in children's mental health and neuroscience, explains that developmental trauma affects the organization of the brain which, in turn, influences the emotional, social, cognitive, and physiological activities of the child. Developmental trauma can range from infant neglect and abuse, dysfunctional households, domestic violence, and alcoholism, to emotionally inconsistent caregivers and lack of important stimuli during the formative years. Unless a child is raised with secure attachments, most likely the percentage of developmental trauma is higher than known. On the other hand, Shock Trauma, also called Trauma with a capital "T," is an emotional response to a terrible event. This is often a single, intense, life-threatening event such as rape, abuse, war, accidents, violence, or natural disasters. Regardless of the event, trauma occurs when the nervous system does not have the ability to process and integrate what is happening. The body's inability to process this somatic experiencing gets registered in the body and alerts the nervous system when similar situations arise.

During our sessions, Mike practiced noticing what else was present for him. His awareness of what happened in his body increased with practice. He could better understand the sequence between the trigger and his reaction. Focusing on himself, his body and mind, allowed Mike to remember that his wife was not just the requests she places. Unless Mike directed his focus with curiosity and kindness to himself, he would get stuck in the loop of old stories, and that is what he expanded—the same old stories. From there, Mike lost a sense of who he was, who his wife was, and what he wanted, along with what else was possible in his life. By keeping his awareness on the present moment, Mike can now zoom in to each part. He can notice his body reactions, hear his thoughts and the meanings being created, and remember that he agreed to the request. Gradually, he can zoom out and see his entire complex self—the full Mike. Focusing on being *here* helps Mike choose his responsibilities. This is principle number three.

Principle 3: Responsibility = Ability to Respond

To be honest, I do not like using the word responsibility. It is a rigid word that carries a heavy burden. The word implies obligations, tasks, and long to-do lists. My mind tenses up with additional demand and with fear of "what if." Rest assured that this is not the connotation I am referring to in this book. For this practice, split the word responsibility in two and reverse its order. Responsibility equals "response" plus "ability." The ability to respond is something much more powerful. This separation of the word brings the focus to who I am and where I am now in the current situation. Responsibility also moves us from reaction to response, from habitual to pondering. When we believe that to be responsible means following certain steps, we become disconnected from what is available in this moment. We reject facts, disregard information, and ignore our own selves. Still, if we were raised to have a script, it would probably take effort to become aware of our internal script.

When we shift to having the ability to respond, we are responsible for how we react in the moment. This perspective considers all that is *here* already: the past, with all its lessons and information, *this* moment now, yourself, and the possible consequences. The present moment is rich and full of possibilities. Personally, I am much more responsible when I ask myself, what is my ability to respond to this as is? This is precisely what happened to Mike. As soon as he noticed what he had been ignoring in himself—his past experiences, the sensations in his body, forgetting the reason he had agreed on certain tasks, his tendency to reduce his wife to a single behavior—Mike started to see what was within his control: his ability to respond. If he was creating the things he was trying to avoid, Mike knew that he could become more aware. He could notice what was possible for him in each moment. I recommended that Mike speak with a therapist if he wanted to look deeper into any childhood traumas. Mike then made a list of what he knew was possible to respond to in his current situation. I reminded Mike that his intention was great and told him that he could have clarity in the moment by assessing his inner world and checking in with his emotions, thoughts, and images of what was happening. He could also look at the meanings he was giving these events. Mike decided on his practice.

On a practical level, we must be informed, trained on a task, and prepared on procedures. We must also understand how the world functions and know our skill level. Life is changing, and the ability to respond to life, to our dance, is not stagnant; it changes according to each of us and what is available in the moment. We dance because we come back to this moment and find out what it is all about and identify where we can take possible action.

Principle 4: Action—Start with
the Smallest Possible Step

Action is part of being alive. People often mistake the invitation of being *here* with doing nothing, and this is not true. I am an advocate of **action, not reaction**. Most of us just react to events in our lives without conscious awareness. Conscious action or purposeful action is imperative to create a better world. Action that is kind and considerate, thoughtful and effective, and mutually beneficial is useful, and above all, healthy. We need to act more but react less. As humans and as part of nature, we are constantly changing. Even if change is invisibly small, it still exits. This is why I recommend we practice conscious action. It might take longer to consider, but the behavior will not just be an unconscious reaction based on what we have learned in the past.

In our industrialized world, whether we agree with it or not, we have been trained to value and expect fast, big, and instant gratification. Collectively, it is difficult to allow and welcome the slow, small steps. Small, in most western cultures, has the connotation of less than, of being impoverished, unimportant, or even infantile. It is as if there is something wrong with practices that suggest small steps. My coaching training showed me how to guide people to think big and to achieve even bigger: big dreams, big visions, big goals. These can also be beneficial in certain situations. I am not defending one approach against the other. Rather, I want to give some relevance to what has been devalued and misrepresented, even if it is being done without our conscious awareness. So, please allow me to focus on the importance of small steps and why we miss out when we ignore them. The most significant achievements happen in small steps.

During a session, Valery was complaining about the chaos in her house. She told me she had unopened boxes from her past two moves in the room she dreamed about turning into her office. However, at this stage in her life she was working full-time and doing her PhD. "I have no time," she told me. Since I do not believe we can manage time—we can only manage the energy we put into the time we have—we turned our focus to the energy this room was taking away from her. I asked Valery how often she thought of these unopened boxes. Valery replied, "All the time." She had clearing the room on her to-do list for two years. She kept planning on taking a weekend off to clear the room, but research, work projects, family, and life always crept into her weekends. A defender of small steps, I invited Valery to give herself fifteen minutes a day, every day. I told her to set a timer, and not allow herself more than that time. We took the first small step during our session together and created a little visualization for the time and emotions Valery wanted to experience. Two weeks later, Valery showed me her room with only a few boxes in a corner. Waiting for a weekend would have been nearly impossible considering her circumstances, but fifteen minutes made this insurmountable project not only doable but rewarding.

The most important aspect of practicing small steps is to shift our focus from the end result to the current circumstances of what is possible. Since the mind projects to the future or to the past, focusing on the body brings us back to this moment so we can find out what smallest step is possible now. Just like driving, we get there by being *here*, by paying attention to the road, the traffic, and the cars in my vicinity. This first small step brings us back to our power, to the process of what is happening right now, to possibilities.

Small steps are our natural design for learning and growing. This first step can seem to take forever; it can feel like giving up. However, the smallest step, even if invisible, is where the magic happens. It is the space that requires us to abandon the ideal way and move in a direction we had not quite imagined. Even more, the smallest step approach frees us to be open, creative, and enjoy this moment. Have you had the experience of getting a big task done once you broke it down into baby steps? Small steps bring us back to what is most natural for our bodies, and we get there with small steps.

Mike decided to take small steps. First, he decided to practice awareness using little mindfulness exercises that would help him notice what he was feeling and thinking. This was the smallest step Mike took. He had a plan for the future as well and focused on the vision of a more loving response to his wife. A relationship in which he felt engaged also helped him come back to presence. His mindfulness practices seemed too small for Mike, and he argued that noticing what was happening with himself would not change anything. I insisted that he play with the practice for a while. Mike did, and he started bringing more and more information about his own internal obstacles, including beliefs he internalized as a child and family sayings that his father used about being a man. The more Mike became aware of his inner world, the more he found ways to respond in the moment. Mike started noticing what would work best for him, such as being more involved and active in voluntarily doing the things he and his wife had agreed upon. Mike told his wife his needs and asked her to say certain things differently. These invisible steps did not solve everything, but they created a more honest way of interacting with his wife. Step by step, Mike knew how to come back *here*, notice the meanings he was giving and where he was focusing, and assess what was possible for him. He had the four principles to help him start again, and so he kept dancing.

The importance of small is not to ignore the vision all together. As with driving, we know where we are heading, but our full attention is on the present moment. This way we are not concerned with what we cannot control but rather with what is ours to notice. The practice of taking small steps creates a win-win-win for the mind, body, and emotions. On an emotional level, the gains are even greater. When the body knows its own emotional sensations, it learns that it is okay to be *here*. It is possible to feel fear, sadness, or anger. Emotions, no matter how unpleasant, are not a threat. The body becomes familiar with the tiny nuances being felt briefly, so it does not react as fast in a fight or flight mode. Small steps allow us to notice what is arising in our bodies gradually. We may feel the discomfort creating inferences, but the more we practice being *here*, the more we gain clarity. This step-by-step, embodied experience of emotions is a key skill to develop. The art of witnessing any escalation gives us the opportunity to know what is best for us in the moment. When I turn to my body and notice where I am emotionally now, I can choose an effective action. The smallest step occurs internally. It is what happens in the body when the music is felt. Be with it!

The advantage of the four principles is not to have a solution to situations, but a guideline to fall back into when our habitual, internalized reactions do not serve us. These principles bring us back to our bodies, to this moment. When we learn something on a step-by-step basis, it gets engraved into our own body memory. It rewires the information, creating new neural pathways in our brains as new learnings are formed. Using a step-by-step process also increases awareness as we become better equipped to notice whether what is being asked is an impulse or whether it reflects our highest intentions. Starting small diminishes fears as we build the confidence to notice our abilities as well as our obstacles, both internal as well as external.

8 ○ ∞

Homeplay: Dancing with the Principles

Do not just take my word for it but play with it yourself. Create your reality, focus on your awareness of what is real and true for you, be responsible for your playtime, and take your first invisible step.

1. Pick an issue or a problem in your life, your "earthquake." It can be a difficult boss, a teenager at home, a health condition, or something relevant for you now. State the facts, just the facts. Ex: My boss yells at everyone.
2. Ask yourself: What are you focusing on? What is expanding?
3. What is your ability to respond to what is happening inside you, the emotions you feel right now? List all that is possible.
4. Look at the list from above. What is the smallest step you can take that would have the biggest impact?
5. Ready for more? Pick another earthquake and start again.

If this exercise is too much for you right now, ask for support and find someone who can be *here* with you. We all need to look someone in the eye and be reminded that this moment can be tough, but we are *here*. I cannot imagine what my life would be like had I not asked for help. No one helped me change facts, but I am constantly reminded that being *here* for this is where I create my reality.

4

Obstacles to The Dance

One of the biggest illusions:
something outside of myself
is going to bring me home.

—JEFF FOSTER

The Obstacles of The Dance
Are Not on The Dance Floor

What are the major obstacles in your life? It took me a tremendous amount of time to understand that I am my biggest obstacle. Humans learn to navigate the physical world from the time they are babies. Before we even decide to move, our five senses identify obstacles in our way. The furniture in our houses becomes an obstacle when we need to walk around. Unless we see it and walk around it, we might hurt ourselves. During mealtime, a table is no longer an obstacle; it becomes a useful asset. It is the same with our emotional and mental obstacles. Contrary to the physical world, I did not learn to move through my emotional and mental world. **Not understanding how my inner world functions became a major obstacle.** A strategy learned as a child to calm the nervous system can be overused to a point of becoming harmful. Depending on the nature of our learned behaviors, our nervous system, and our emotional baggage, we may be stuck in strategies or old habits that have turned into addictions. These misuses or abusing habits may be our greatest obstacles.

More than the external constraints of natural disasters, finances, traffic, and difficult people, our own inner abilities to navigate life can be obstacles. Just like with external obstacles, the possibilities of what can be internal obstacles are endless. It is impossible to be prepared for them all. However, there are common patterns and ways that, once known, will no longer make us stumble and fall. Emotionally, I spent seemingly endless years and a fortune in therapy trying to eliminate the obstacles. Instead of dancing life, I spent time and energy dragging furniture around, rearranging, and cleaning the floor. What I found through therapy, coaching, and trial and error is that I can feel empowered by getting to see what is happening inside of me, coming closer to my own learnings, and making room for what is occurring in my present experience. This shift has made the difference. I already do this on a dance floor; I look around, identify where everything is, and dance in the space I have. This chapter highlights four obstacles I know well and frequently see in my practice. These are fighting life, prostituting myself to meet my needs, struggling with addictions, and being stuck in older versions of myself. What will your dance look like once you know your obstacles?

1. Fighting Life

Mary was referred to me by her doctor. She was a recently divorced, educated, and caring mother of two. Mary asked for help to cope with the demanding transitions she was experiencing. As Mary shared her situation, I felt her vulnerability and strength. She showed great love for her children, and she felt fear for the future she wanted for them. My heart broke with every word I heard. Mary had many unanswered questions, two girls to care for, school payments to make, an ex who was unwilling to step up to his role as a father, finances to sort out, a house to run, daily logistics to manage, and a demanding job. How would she do it all? Tears rolled down Mary's face. I cherished that moment because I sensed that crying was not an easy thing for Mary to allow herself to do, let alone to cry in front of a stranger. I recognized myself in her story and thought, "I know this fight."

Do you fight life? I am a fighter myself, so much so that Stop Fighting, Start Living was the first e-book I wrote for Upanji's website. Like most of my self-work, the book started with a long, comprehensive list so I could make each entry more tangible. Fighting had been such a large part of my life that **I had to know more about why I fought and the purpose it served in my life.** In my experiences, I learned that fighting life is an inability to see beyond the obvious. I was unable to see beyond the immediate sensation, the natural reactive alarm signals firing up in my nervous system in the body. The obvious is happening. However, when I am unaware, what is happening in my body is not so clear. When we say "It was so obvious anyone could see it," we often forget that we all see differently according to who and where we are at the moment. So, seeing beyond the obvious implies being aware that what we see is based on our own abilities to see and be in this moment. What allows us to see is a combination of our previous experiences, training, and culture, along with the strategies we learned along the way. Although true, these variables are only a part of what we learned, and there is more; there is the part that is fixed and a part of our original design.

As humans, our reptilian brain is naturally designed to protect us. It holds a primal, instinctive mechanism for survival, and it reacts to any perceived threat with fight, flight, or freeze responses. When this primitive protective mode is triggered, we do not have many options. Our instincts are set to reject, refuse, and deny alternatives because we need to react fast. The instinctive design is perfect for when the threat is a real life or death situation. For example, if a wild animal attacks us, we should fight. However, unless we are literally about to physically die, it is important to learn practices that allow us to stop and notice rather than react in a primitive way. As we pay attention to how we use this reptilian brain, we start to see that most of the time our fight or flight gets activated on perceived threats rather than actual threats. Even when we are not being attacked physically, we can perceive change or emotional discomfort as a threat. In the example above, the threat was a divorce. A divorce is a big change in life that can trigger the nervous system into a fight or flight response. Other everyday situations can have the same effect, such as the loss of a job or a bill to pay. Sometimes, simply having someone disagree with our opinion can be perceived as a threat. Triggers can also be unfamiliar situations or something new such as a move or an interview. All the above are not imminent death threats. These are emotional challenges, but no one dies because of them.

The first time I was able to notice myself experiencing an emotional reaction that I was perceiving as a threat was with my husband. He was reading the news and made a comment that triggered me. I cannot even remember the actual words, but I remember what I felt in my body. There was this fire-like ball rising inside my belly, moving up, resembling an explosion. Meanwhile, in my head, thoughts fired up sentences to rebut his comment. The argument was playing itself out; I was relentlessly talking at him, as I do in such situations, and I was agitated, pointing my finger, angrily saying, "How dare you say such a stupid thing." In my head I was aggressive and personal. I got up and stormed out of the room. Remarkably, the funny fact was that all this reactive commotion was only happening inside my head. I was noticing it. I was still silently sitting down. Previously, I had been able to see triggers in retrospect, but this was the first time I was able to notice, in real time, what a trigger ignited inside of me. I was aware, in real time. This time, however, the difference was that I did not act on it. I did not yell at my husband. I was noticing my own emotions, thoughts, and impulses enticing me to protect myself. My husband looked at me, and he must have noticed something because he asked, "What?" First, my answer was "Nothing." But I noticed I could speak now, so I explained that what he said had triggered me. We talked about it, and I reminded him of what I feel as a woman who grew up in a misogynist environment. Looking back, I know his comment was not offensive nor inappropriate, but my nervous system is conditioned by my past to be on the watch-out and be ready to attack—a good example of how old strategies can become unhealthy. This practice of being *here* is beneficial as it helps us detect the difference between a life threat and emotional discomfort in our bodies.

Have you been in a similar situation? Maybe you get nervous before an exam. You might sweat, and you start thinking of ways to escape. Unless learned and trained, our own nervous system can misinterpret emotional pain and discomfort as a threat to our survival. As soon as the body experiences these sensations, it signals a loud "Get me out!" to the brain and activates a fight, flight, or freeze response. We get ourselves into trouble when we fight for our survival without being physically in danger. We start viewing change as a threat, uncertainty as a threat, and suddenly, someone else's opinion is felt as an attack. Our bodies then respond as if we are about to die. The mind asks a question like, "How am I going to pay my bills?" and the heart races, pupils dilate, and our body goes into fight or flight. The fight does not ask permission or want our input. It is up to us to turn to ourselves and understand how we work. This requires seeing beyond our own instinctive mechanism. Slowly, we can learn new ways to get to know what is possible before we are triggered. By opening up to other possibilities, we see that we have choices. We can choose to fight if and only when needed. Fighting life is fighting our inner world, our natural make up, and that is futile and exhausting.

Mary shared her life before was not perfect but was functional. With two adults in the house, completing the required tasks and obligations had already been difficult; how would she cope now? Her girls were involved in extracurricular activities. How would they manage now that they had a single mom who was pressed for time? Why couldn't her husband just grow up and step up? Why couldn't he help with swimming, music lessons, soccer for one, basketball for the other, or any other important activities for the girls' development? Why couldn't he be reasonable? Mary beat herself up by saying, "I should have known he would be like this. If before, I could only play golf once a week, it will be another 10 years until I can play again. What about the expenses? What if I get sick?" I could feel Mary's pain and see her struggling to even imagine a different possibility. Her mind was looking for what was familiar and worked in the past. Mary was feeling the added burden of tasks, the natural uncertainty and emotional discomfort that had stemmed from her divorce.

We Cannot Rehearse for Life

Do you stress out when something does not go according to plan? According to the Holmes and Rahe[13] stress scale, divorce ranks second on the top ten most stressful events in life. These stressful situations impact our nervous system. We know that being prepared can diminish our stress. However, mistaking preparedness for tasks with preparedness for life is the easiest way to displace our energy. We can plan, and it is important to feel prepared by getting organized, recruiting support for the school runs, or asking for help with children's extracurricular activities. Likewise, we can create plans for grocery shopping, cooking, managing money, paying bills, taking children to school on time, and showing up for work. Although these preparations are helpful, we cannot erroneously expect to control everything. We prepare to reduce stress but then, unless everything is running accordingly, our nervous system continues to be triggered by feeling even more stress. This is what I mean when I say we cannot prepare for life. For example, we can drive but we cannot anticipate or control the flow of traffic. It is a waste of our energy to want traffic to be different or drivers to behave differently.

As a self-assumed "control freak in recovery," I have always wanted to ensure results, to control. This has been my mistake. Instead of keeping my hands on the wheel and eyes on the road, I wanted traffic to flow at my will. As a result, I would become stressed out and angry with most everything in my life. I still do this when I am not mindful. Each one of my many moves (and when I move it seems I move to another country), have shown me my need to control. My plans and strategies, my constant preparation, and my wanting to know everything ahead made it so I could not sleep well. I packed everything in order, with lists outside and inside, made copies, and saved them in different places. The details of how everything SHOULD work was overwhelming, and all it took was seeing the movers load one of my boxes upside down and all hell would break loose. When I started practicing these tools, I became aware of this distinction: planning how I would pack usefully but wanting the move to happen the way I had mentally rehearsed was impossible. That was fighting life. In my last two moves, I did not even do the packing myself. I hired a company to do it, and I purposefully arranged to be busy that day. No rehearsal, just simple, logistic, useful, practical lists. I spent the rest of my time being *here*, noticing my own nervous system, and being aware of what was possible in each moment.

When I am present, I see the distinction between what I can prepare for in life and what I cannot control. To avoid making the same mistakes, I had to learn to see each one separately and understand how these two aspects are linked. One aspect included driving or packing, specific tasks on which I needed to act. The other aspect was the idea that the movers should work the way I wanted them to and in a way over which I had control. Confusion arises when I do not notice which is which and attribute an emotional meaning to the mover's work. I feel my system yelling, "Get me out!" The illusion is that traffic is creating my discomfort and the fighting begins. My practice shows me that **I am better off using my energy finding ways to be *here*.** As I practice turning inward and noticing my nervous system in this discomfort, I find what is possible for me now. If there is something I need to do, then I act, even if this means fighting for my survival. Knowing the distinction has helped me reduce my learned behavior of fighting life itself. There is no need to rehearse steps for a dance for which I cannot predict the music.

The Fighting Blueprint

Do you fight life? Twenty years ago, if asked, I would have said I do not fight life. I make things happen, which means I am strong, prepared, and informed. I would offer up whatever excuse was true for me at the time. The truth is that I was both fighting and not fighting life at the same time. It took me another ten years to realize this distinction, and another ten to rewrite a new format. It is my purpose and source of joy to share my gains with you. The following is a list of my insights and what I learned in the process:

I fight Life when I:

1. Resist change
2. Focus on what is missing
3. Expect others to behave in a certain way
4. Want my personal rules to be *the* rule
5. Believe I am the same as I was yesterday
6. Say "I Should"
7. Compare myself to others
8. Live in the past or future
9. Am not true to myself as I am *here now*
10. Avoid acting on what I know is for me
11. Want to be right
12. Get stuck in the problem ...

Sometimes we start fighting life at such a young age that we develop a fighting blueprint. When I first wrote *Stop Fighting, Start Living*, I remember debating my mind's arguments telling me that each of these rules has an important role to protect me and keep me safe. Although this is true, there is a catch. Once the blueprint is installed, we fight first and mostly everything. Change is inevitable, and when it happens, we can feel emotions we do not enjoy feeling. We use all our energy trying to change what is visible—circumstances, things, others. What really needs attention is the underlying emotional state that is uncomfortable with the change. Using an example of one of my first adult moves, I see that even though I chose and wanted to move, my fighting-life mode was on. Now, I can see what I did not know then. The list above was serving to avoid the underlying emotions around my move: the uncertainty of the new life ahead, the fear of losing some irreplaceable sentimental objects, missing friends and the life I had built already. I kept fighting with every detail. I argued that the boxes did not have the exact right size for what I needed, with the store attendant who did not notice I needed assistance, or with anyone who crossed my path. What practicing being *here* has given me is noticing the distinctions between the underlying emotion and the action itself. This listening to the system screaming is great, but it requires practice to notice before the "get me out" takes over.

What is your blueprint? The term comes from engineering, and it refers to a process that allows rapid reproduction of copies. What I learned over the years is that behaviorally we develop a blueprint based on our early experiences. Repetition accelerates the reaction times and strengthens the blueprint. It becomes automatic, which is why the trigger appears. It is so fast that no other choices seem available. Our bodies reinforce our blueprint with sensations of discomfort. Signals keep firing up and we are stuck in the loop. In the reactive loop stage, it is physically impossible to stop and notice that the blueprint is reacting on our behalf. Although this is what we have learned so far, it is possible to learn other ways of responding, which is just what Mary did. After we reviewed the four major coaching principles, Mary began practicing with reclaiming her power. The first small step was to turn to herself and explore what was possible in her situation. The mornings were tough, and it was difficult to get her girls to school on time because there was so much to prepare in the morning. How does she want to feel while driving the girls to school in the morning? Instead of focusing on what was going wrong or not ready, like the traffic or the clock ticking, Mary started noticing what was happening in her body. She connected with her emotions and decided to get to know her fighting mode. She noticed all her concerns and fears and was ready to focus on the mother she wanted to be emotionally. Mary stated she wanted to be present and engaged in conversation instead of being stressed and on edge.

After a few attempts, Mary announced that on a rushed morning they were leaving the house and were already late for school. Mary noticed her learned behavior kick in—her agitation and self-blaming thoughts in her head, her desire to yell at traffic and the world. She anticipated her children being reprimanded in school for tardiness again, which made her feel like she was failing as a mother. The traffic light turned red, and she remembered to turn to herself and focus on her breathing and who she wanted to be. She noticed herself getting calmer. When the light turned green, Mary continued to focus on the present moment and reminded herself that here she could relax, keep her eyes on the road, breathe a little bit deeper, and continue to engage in conversation with her children. We had talked extensively about the mother she wanted to be, how she felt when she was that mother, and what could help her remember those images and sensations. Against all odds, they arrived at school on time. Mary had tasted the benefits of the pausing practice. Whether they managed to get there on time or not, Mary had been present and did her best, which was all she could do.

Today, Mary's dance is flowing. She is still divorced and still has the same physical tasks that are difficult to manage at times. Mary is aware of her old fighting blueprint and the importance of being with herself and her circumstances. Every now and then we cross paths, and Mary looks a lot happier. She chats away about sneaking off to play golf whenever she can and about joining a supportive community of like-minded friends. She even occasionally manages to attend a play. By accepting her daughter's father for who he is, Mary changed the way she communicates with him, and when she asks, he is sometimes more available and involved in their lives. To Mary's credit, her consistent small steps have paid off. By turning to herself and accepting her fighting blueprint, she catches herself when she falls back into the habitual old pattern. *Here*, Mary is her own best friend, and through her inner peace, her girls gained a more relaxed, playful, and engaged mother. No, she does not have the time to do all that she wishes she could, but Mary makes the most with what she has. Mary is choosing her own dance style by focusing on what is possible as opposed to becoming stressed out when others do not step up as they should.

Do you fight life? Fighting is natural, and it can be beneficial, which is why we have the instinctive impulse to do it. A certain level of fighting energy is healthy for action and setting boundaries. However, fighting life can rob us of aliveness and options, which can hurt us. When we can identify our own instinctive or unconscious learned strategies, we feel empowered. We then choose how to dance in the moment. An embodied self-awareness practice helps us see the many ways we have learned to ignore ourselves and even "sell out" what is true for us.

2. Prostituting Ourselves to Meet Our Needs

My sister sits at a table staring at her plate as if she was condemned to forced labor. I learned a lot about what was expected and what was rewarded by my parents just by observing my sister. My parents were happier with empty plates, when no questions were asked, and when there was no fuss. I must have been about four years old when I learned to hide my fear. Sometimes after dinner my father would realize he had run out of cigarettes. He would ask one of us to run to the bedroom to get him a pack. I always volunteered out of my need to impress him, but also because I had already finished eating. Besides, I knew my sister was afraid of the dark. Even though I shared the same fear, I did not believe fear was a valued emotion. So, I learned to both omit and disguise my fear, or better said, to lie.

I use the above story to highlight a couple of obstacles we face when learning to accept life's invitations to dance. Unconsciously, we learn to "prostitute" ourselves on an emotional level. Yes, this is a strong word, but it makes the concept easier to explain. Acculturation is a necessary process for humans to learn to coexist and be safe, but it has its side effects. Somewhere along the way of learning language and shared behaviors, we also learn to ignore our truth. This happens through no fault of our own nor of those around us, but still, it happens and is an important obstacle to acknowledge.

As children, we unconsciously learn through interaction with others. We scan the world with our senses and give meanings to what we gather, according to the ability of our receptors and our tender nervous system. At the age of four, I heard my mother tell my sister to finish her food, but I did not understand all the implications. I knew nothing about nutrition or energy and could not understand the reasons why my mother would tell my sister to eat. As I repeatedly watched my sister struggle with food, my body registered what I saw and how I felt about it. I tried to make sense of the experience. At that moment, just looking at my sister was uncomfortable, so I experienced discomfort. I registered the sensation as a physical threat in my system, which told me that this is a situation I should avoid because I did not want to feel that way. So, I found a solution and learned to eat fast. My mother approved my behavior and gave me a compliment, so I repeated the behavior and learned from the experience. However, this solution never addressed my emotional discomfort. I did not learn to pay attention to myself and observe what happened for me when I ate fast or slow. I did not stop to determine whether I was satisfied or not, or whether my discomfort changed.

We learn the obstacles to dancing life at the level of a child's ability. Unless we are supported to turn inwards, we learn to ignore our truth. Hence my use of the term "prostitution." We "sell" whatever is here for us, searching for a quick fix that rarely addresses the emotion itself. The quick fix is an escape from the unpleasant to a pleasant sensation, whatever that is for us at the time. As a child, I did not want to risk being in my sister's position, which felt too painful to bear. It would be threatening to not have my parent's approval, like my sister at the dinner table. I learned to avoid this threat even if it meant ignoring my own fears of the dark to get my father's cigarettes.

I take off running. At the first glimpse of darkness, I close my eyes, open my arms to touch a wall for guidance, and hold my breath. My imagination runs wild with all sorts of monsters. I let my hands guide me in the dark as I get a pack of cigarettes and run back. I hold my breath the whole time. Giving my father his cigarettes is the highlight of my day—his half smile, his eyes on me, his comment on how fast I run. As my heart heavily pounds, I get the most terrifying thought. The thought is even scarier than monsters catching up to me–what if my father could tell I was indeed afraid?

What We Carry on The Dance Floor:
Learning Awareness

As you read the above story, did you feel I was rough using the word "prostitution" for a young girl? It is easy to say, "No harm done, you were only four," which is true. But when we remain unaware of what emotional needs these behaviors serve, we will continue to reproduce them throughout our adult life. If a lie gives me the recognition, approval, and attention I need, I will remember and repeat that lie. As children we also learn schemas. Jean Piaget, the Swiss psychologist known for his theory of cognitive development, defines schemas[14] as a cognitive framework that helps us organize and make sense of the information we gather. Once I learned to sell my truth for recognition or love, I began to carry that schema. I kept the framework, which is reinforced each time it happens. Relationships that function primary on pervasive negative verbal exchange, a hostile insecure environment, addiction, abuse, and infidelity in adult intimate relationships can often be traced back to learned childhood dynamics. This is why it is important to become aware of our inner world and our emotional needs and how we have learned to fulfill these needs. Our old schemas are useful because they facilitate the learning process, but when we become complacent, our schemas can prevent a new healthier response.

Awareness is most important at this stage. By developing a practice to turn to ourselves and identify our unmet emotional needs, we become able to make conscious choices. It takes time to first assimilate what is new and then persist in challenging our old ways. Awareness on its own is not enough, but we cannot address the issue until we become aware of what we carry. We must accept our learned schemas to identify when the learned behavior is an obstacle or when it is useful. In this way, we dance between the comfort of the familiar and the challenge of the new. Change requires effort and practice. This is what turns assimilation of the new information and behavior into an accommodation for an updated schema that we can use daily.

We can excuse our younger selves for what and how we learned. However, we learn behaviors that meet our most basic human needs. Feeling safe, being autonomous, feeling love and belonging, a sense of having value, being seen and recognized— these needs are the driving force of a child's behavior. I wish I could go back in time and tell my younger self that she is safe, that my parents would never abandon her. She is already accepted and loved no matter what. I would tell her that her mother's teachings were about preparing her for the world, not a sign of disapproval of who she is. Now, as an adult, I see how easily I learned to ignore my truth and hide my dance. Had I learned to recognize and accept all my emotions, I would have learned to notice my fear for what it was. I would have acknowledged that my needs are natural, and I would have grown up closer to myself rather than running away from how I felt. Seeing what is *here* allows us to dance among what is possible. Are you aware of how you have learned to meet your most basic needs? By being aware of our emotional needs, we can also prevent the repetitive behaviors that often lead us into addictions, which is another frequent obstacle to our dance.

3. Addictions: Seeing Beyond the Drunk

The foul vomitous odors of a drinking night still lingered on the sidewalks by the pubs. I am running late for my Saturday

7 a.m. yoga class, when I see a stumbling drunk man turning the corner. I look at him and think the worst. I imagine him vomiting just as we pass by one another. I catch my thoughts and question my judgements. I believe that what I see is about me, so I ask myself: What am I really seeing? I see an inability to experience some emotions, a man unconsciously trying everything to not face the music of his life. I see fear and a desperate cry for help. I see a man running away from his true self. I see old patterns, old habits, and learned steps repeating themselves, which he likely had for generations before him. Now, I can relate. Drinking is not my addiction, but I know the unconscious running away from myself. I pass the man with a heart full of compassion and a renewed respect for our human condition. I know that old habits not only numb us but keep us stuck in this repeated addictive dance.

What is an *addiction* and why does it matter? We cannot choose to dance (at least not consciously) when we are unaware of what driving forces guide our choices and behaviors. I am using the following definition: *Addiction* is "a strong inclination to do, use, or indulge in something repeatedly." *Addiction* feels like having a broken record inside. Until we understand the underlying reasons for our strong inclinations, we cannot be fully autonomous. According to the definition, we are all addicted to something. Many of us do not see our addictions as such because they can be cultural or generational. Addictions include things such as sugar, caffeine, work, and exercise, all of which are socially acceptable. Therefore, it is harder to draw the line between healthy use and *addiction*. It is up to each one of us to notice our level of use or abuse. However, many of us know we are addicted and refuse to admit it by excusing the behavior as beneficial, which can be true at times. *Addiction* is a complex and well-studied field, and I am no expert in it. However, as a coach with nearly 20 years of experience, I study the importance of being aware of our obstacles for our overall well-being. Since we already know that we tend to be our greatest obstacles with any goal, it is crucial to identify the driving forces that create our obstacles. Knowing our *addictions* allows us greater awareness of ourselves as well as the ability to create possibilities with what is at our disposal. It can be empowering to understand our own addictive patterns.

The Root Cause

How does an *addiction* start? Let us create a sort of inner contact tracing of signals until we get to the first step. What is most relevant is that we can be addicted to anything that physically creates the neuron connections and chemical reactions in our bodies. This is what drives us to want to repeat and enforces a choice. *Addictions* can start as healthy or unhealthy. More than the substance itself or even the behavior, it is the invisible inner pattern that matters most and often it did not start with us.[15] For the purpose of this inner experience, we ask ourselves what started the whole chain of connections. The root leads us to the emotional need, which is a driving force of it all.

Do you crave sugar sometimes? Let us use sugar as an example. Sugar was my first *addiction*; it is a chemical substance and has emotional associations. It was the associations I made between sugar and feeling a certain emotion that hooked me. What emotional meaning does this experience have? When I was young, I did not like sweet treats. I would rather have salty and crunchy. Sweets were for celebrations, special occasions, and rewards. As a child I might not have liked sweets, but I wanted to celebrate, to be rewarded. First, I would eat just to join in, then sugar did the rest. I started to associate sugar with celebration and the memories became stored in my body saying, "I know this, and it makes me feel good." The memory is felt as pleasant. Pleasant sensations make us feel safe, seen, and loved. We do not do this consciously. It makes sense that, when and if we need to feel any of those emotions, we unconsciously repeat that behavior. As humans, we are designed to avoid pain and discomfort and look for pleasure. Now, put this natural tendency on repeat and it creates a habit.

Do you want to break a habit? A habit loop is a pattern that consists of three steps. First it needs a cue, then a routine, and then it must create a reward. The cue can be a place, person, or time of day. A cue signals the brain to want a substance or an experience. Every time I pass the corner pastry shop, I have to go in and buy a cinnamon roll. Rewards are also not so straightforward and can be the pleasure of stopping, sugar itself, or an associated memory with cinnamon rolls. Identifying a habit loop takes some investigation. Being curious about what makes me do certain things has been a life saver. Being unaware of what is underneath my choices can make room for harmless habits to become addictions.

The line between a habit and an addiction is not always clear. Three factors are used to diagnose an *addiction*: the amount of time or quantity spent, the chemical reactions in the brain, and withdrawal symptoms. Human brains do not respond equally to substances and experiences. What makes one brain all fired up might make someone else's brain have no reaction. This seems to be the main reason some people can have a habit and never become addicted while others need to keep going back for more. The amount required to create the same sensations also increases with use. Another thing to lookout for is the withdrawal symptoms. If I cannot function, cannot stop thinking about my cinnamon roll, or shake when I do not get my sugar fix, I might be addicted. The chemical reaction also determines *addiction* as a disease that needs more than a change of habit to be addressed. As I mentioned before, my interest in addiction is much more related to understanding the root cause of *addiction* then the addiction itself. Personally, I notice that focusing on the *addiction* drives me to either go deeper into it or find disorganized compensations. What seems to work and be important overall is to become aware of my own patterns. I included the topic of *addiction* in this book because it is important for me to know the obstacles to my dance. I do not know if you relate, but all my addictions came from an emotional state, an unmet need, and my inability to self-regulate. Embodied self-awareness, this practice of being *here*, has been what gives me room to listen to the music playing. I see the behavior, get curious, notice the inner fight, the judgements, the sensations in my body and with small steps, move to the best of my ability.

Comprehensive Approach to Dance

Addiction is a complex problem starting with the fact that most people who have an *addiction* do not recognize it as such. Awareness, therefore, can be a useful step in the process of accepting it is a problem. Once an *addiction* is recognized, it is important to identify the level of support that is required for each person. *Addictions* have many components, including physical, mental, emotional, spiritual, social, and occupational. *Addictions* deserve a comprehensive approach too. Collectively, we need to remove the taboos and humanize *addiction* while addressing and tackling the many issues from several fronts. In 2016, The Comprehensive Addiction and Recovery Act (CARA)[16] established "a comprehensive, coordinated, balanced strategy through enhanced grant programs that would expand prevention and education efforts while also promoting treatment and recovery." CARA encompasses six pillars: prevention, treatment, recovery, law enforcement, criminal justice reform, and overdose reversal. According to the National Center for Drug Abuse Statistics, "In 2018, 53 million or 19.4% of people aged 12 years and older used illegal drugs or misused prescription drugs in the previous year." When alcohol and tobacco are included, this number jumps to 60.2 percent or 165 million people. Is it just me, or did you also dismiss these numbers with some thought like, "Not everyone who uses illegal drugs has an *addiction*"? Or did you deflect and say that these are the hard-core addicts, not most people and certainly not you? I caught myself thinking this and had to remember that what is important is awareness. Regardless of the specifics of every situation, millions of people are attempting to regulate their nervous system with these substances. I might not use illegal drugs, drink, or smoke, but what about self-harm, caffeine, binge-watching, computer games, Internet surfing, social media, food, shopping, pornography, sex, work…? In 2020[17] the report *Evidence Based Strategies for Abatement of Harms from the Opioid Epidemic* joined several experts to recommend strategies to end the opioid crisis. Chapter two starts by stating, "Programs that offer the greatest number of evidence-based components (medications, behavioral therapies, and recovery support services) tend to have the greatest likelihood of facilitating recovery." The reason I am most interested in awareness is because I accept there are no panaceas. Therefore, it is important to see the big picture (the root cause) that feeds the addictive cycle. Humans are complex and *addictions* are not our fault but are an obstacle to our dance.

Fred came to see me asking for help to save his marriage. His wife had attended one of my workshops and had mentioned me. He just wanted the result, which was to keep his family together. Fred loved his wife and children, and he knew he needed to do something drastic to convince his wife to stay. First, Fred accused his wife of nit-picking and being a perfectionist who is always overwhelmed with the children's needs, the house, her work, and her elderly parents. I listened carefully and asked how her behavior was creating a problem for him. Fred started listing the things he did to fix her. I asked him, if he had to say what needs his wife was meeting with all her behaviors, what would he guess. His first answer was that she nags him because she needs support. He said he just did not have time, so we explored possibilities. Fred needed many sessions, with many cancelations in between, to confess an important fact about himself. He kept trying to fix his wife, his marriage, and his family dynamic, but the cause of the problem was his addiction to sex. He spoke about just forgetting everything for a while, not thinking of anything at all. These women were nothing more than a vehicle to help him not feel what he felt constantly. His wife caught him many times and forgave him, but things got worse each time. Fred felt even more guilty and ashamed of himself, which meant he diminished the time he was home. Fred's *addiction* was a major obstacle not just for his marriage, but for the life he told me he wanted to live.

Life's dance requires an all-inclusive, comprehensive approach. We must include our needs, our emotions, and the meanings we give to the experiences. In Fred's experience, the addiction started with porn when he was a teenager. However, it did not start there because his emotional needs were not being met before that. His parents had a nasty divorce when he was young, hence the fear of causing the same to his two preteen boys. When Fred had his first encounter with porn, he learned to release tension. Naturally, releasing tension with porn became a habit that was more than exploring his sexual sensations. He first had sex at the age of 14 and sex became his means to regulate his overloaded nervous system. Being overly sexually active made him feel good physically, emotionally, and socially as he gained approval and admiration from his peers. The rewards were many.

Addiction is an interpersonal, neurobiological process for always trying to solve a problem. That is why I believe that any approach to *addiction* needs kindness toward our human condition. We can see beyond the experience itself, noticing the associations in the brain, remembering the sensations, and doing anything to increase awareness. When we turn to ourselves rather than just blame the person or the behavior or substance, we can see ourselves and how we are feeding the cycle. There is no blame intended here, and what matters is that we recognize the *addiction* beyond the substances. The body keeps score, and the root cause of an *addiction* is buried in our unconscious with the connections we established sometimes long before this moment. When we are young, our ability to give meaning is appropriate to our age. I asked Fred to look for a more in-depth comprehensive approach to help him address the root cause of his young nervous system. I suggested he started with Somatic

Experiencing or EMDR to look at the possible trauma from his parents' relationship and divorce. Our capacity to experience life with its pains and discomforts can be compromised because we cannot fully make sense of our experiences. We might not all need a recovery program for our *addictions*, but we are better equipped to overcome life's hurdles once we have paused to understand our *addictions*. Just like on the dance floor, our dance flows better when we identify and learn to deal with the obstacles in the room.

Turning Toward

Are you asking me to turn toward my obstacles? Yes. Until we turn towards what is there, we will continue to trip over them. Start from far, from a safe space. First observe, notice, and identify your addictions. I have to keep dismantling my perception of *addiction* and remind myself that *addiction* is "a strong inclination to do, use, or indulge in something repeatedly." My question is, what is pulling me toward this? It can be a substance that may be perceived as healthy. For example, I was *addicted* to almonds. Seriously, I would hide almonds around the house, every one of my coats had almonds in its pockets, and I would not go anywhere without almonds. Once I noticed and I mentioned my addiction, people would dismiss it saying, "But almonds are healthy." Almonds might be healthy, but my behavior was not. I noticed myself addicted to an ideal or a cause obsessed with one way, one belief, and refusing blindly any fact that would even bring that ideal to less than the perfect image I had created—like a kid refusing to hear the truth about Santa. What makes me follow this group? What behaviors

73

do I engage in and feel drawn to repeat? What social trends touch me deeply? This is safe to observe; it is pure curiosity, a first encounter with who am I *here*. In my experience, small, consistent steps are key to support my ability to notice and learn to be with myself. It takes a healthy nervous system to withhold our multilayered human condition.

What is underneath all my obstacles? In this moment, can we identify the sensation or emotion that we want to escape? On the surface, it might seem like we are just looking for a high or a release. What needs drive our desire for a high? What are we not wanting to feel? There is likely a discomfort, and this discomfort screams for a way out. The brain starts working incessantly to fulfill its wishes. Brain plasticity[18] has shown that our brain changes with experiences. The overstimulation of the brain caused by an *addiction* changes the brain chemistry and sets a new standard of what to aim for. New neural pathways are formed as signaling adapts to the new *addiction* and screams for more. This brain effect explains why addicts get that distinctive look, the narrow focus on the next high. Parents of teenagers describe this look when they try to get them off their screens. The communication patterns change, and these changes affect other regions of the brain. Recovering addicts and their families talk about impaired decision making, uncharacteristic impulsive behaviors, followed by compulsion and cravings and denial that there is a problem. Even tough addictions require a comprehensive approach. The first step is to turn toward it and be curious.

Renowned teacher of comparative mythology, Joseph Campbell, invites us to be brave and curious. His popular quotes states, "The cave you fear to enter holds the treasures you seek."[19] This is the invitation to turn toward the music, slowly, with support and kindness. Gradually, we learn to face the discomfort that our nervous systems learned to avoid. The highs serve to disguise the discomfort. Getting to know our discomfort gives us information for what is possible. This discomfort can have many faces because causes of *addiction* are as individual as we are. Turning toward what is possible *here* is the first step to see what is there. It can be an emotional pain or depression, a feeling of inadequacy, or a sense of not feeling safe, not belonging, or not being enough. Perhaps it is fear that who we are will never be loved. This underlying discomfort rarely goes away, and no substance will get rid of it, so we better get closer. When we stop to observe, we can notice before reacting to relieve our emotional distress. Little by little, as we brave the cave of the unknown to the level of our ability in each moment, we engage in a different behavior. In the same way we became addicted, we create the possibility of another response. Facing what is *here* and entering the cave might reveal the exact sensation that we are seeking. The music playing might be the same, nonetheless we become a little more attuned to what is driving us.

4. Being Stuck in Older Versions

I am nearly six years old, but not yet in school. I am visiting my grandparents, and this means going to the store and getting ice cream with my grandmother. One cone, one "escudo" (a large dark coin, the only one I know and ever used). My grandfather gives me a smaller silver coin, two fifty escudos. Instinctively, I refuse it as I know that it is not my coin. My grandfather laughs. I feel confused and wronged. The black coin gives me ice cream, this is my certainty. My grandfather tells me that this coin is enough, but I do not trust his information. My older sister readily offers to give me her one escudo coin. I refuse. I do not want to feel that she does not get her ice cream because of me. She says my coin is of a greater value. Now I am lost. I thought she was sacrificing for me. Still, I remain fixated on my larger coin, the one I want. I feel stuck. Annoyed, I take the coin. Getting to the store, showing my coin and not saying a word, I doubt I will get ice cream. To my astonishment, I not only get my ice cream, but I also get the change of two coins. I am overjoyed. Now I get it! Now I understand what everyone had been telling me.

Can you relate? Have you ever felt stuck on old perceptions and fought for your limitations? In this example, I was stuck in my old experience. I refused to change, fighting the facts because my body had registered something different from what was being presented. I got stuck on what I knew as true. I use a child as the main character of this story because it makes it easier to remain open to our human inabilities and to see beyond the familiar. Nevertheless, regardless of age, humans create their realities in this exact same way. As with our physical bodies, we can only hear the music according to our hearing abilities. In general, we only receive the information that our system is already capable of receiving. It is as if we have a filter, and this filter has the shape of our previous experiences. If what we are seeing does not fit into our filter, we either reject it or force it to fit. The facts might be true, but the way we receive the facts is altered by our previous learnings. In this silly story, I did not know much about coins and refused what was not my reference, my black coin. Even when my grandfather and sister tried to help me, I was unable to comprehend. The new information did not fit the shape of my filter. My template filter told me I only get ice cream this one way. I was so stuck that I could not even question my experience as not exclusive. This was an obstacle in my six-year-old life. Where else in my life am I doing just that?

The Unquestioned Meanings

In this story, my young version gave several meanings to the facts all based on my previous experience. Meaning one: only one coin could get me an ice cream. Meaning two: without that coin, I would miss out on my ice cream. Meaning three: my grandfather was mistaken or was not telling me the truth. Meaning four: my sister was sacrificing for me (something familiar in my life). Meaning five: I was being made fun of. Meaning six: the world was against me. Meaning seven: I would get to the ice cream shop and be embarrassed for not having the right coin. Meaning eight: I finally understood, and the truth became clear. The new experience became my new template. Once we have a new experience and add another level of understanding, we view life through a new perspective. Each meaning I gave to my experience was associated with an emotion. As soon as I thought, "I will not have my ice cream," I felt lost. My body experienced these emotions as soon as I had created the meaning in my mind. I literally created my reality. I created the meaning, the meaning was received physiologically and felt in sensations that created the emotions, and together this was what I was experiencing. I tensed up, felt fear, confusion, and frustration. My two main obstacles included the meaning I assigned to the coin and not being self-aware. No one was against me; no one was doing anything to me. I had done it all by myself. I was totally hearing impaired and refused a hearing aid even when I was being given one. Instead, I looked at everyone dancing thinking they were all crazy. When we are unaware of how our experiences condition our abilities, we are less capable of noticing how the chain reaction creates meaning. We cannot see how we are creating our own obstacles.

Question Certainty

I did not like the realization that what I see is conditioned by my previous experiences. What? I cannot blame my grandfather for giving me the wrong coin? This realization was a game changer, and it changed my coaching practice. I could not continue to help people create goals when most of us are not aware that we are creating goals that are limiting our lives. Goals are great, and even greater when we see that what we want is the dance. Unless we question the original certainty, which has often been internalized during our early development, the goal we want to create will not reflect the life we want to live. It is as if we had been taught a traditional dance and refused any other dance styles. We need to go beyond this fixed perception that there is only one way to dance. This is the reason I started using the Deathbed Exercise for clarity in finding this unique *Selfprint*, this ability to create something unique together with the music. We all have this uniqueness. Once we touch what is true and matters to us, then we can apply the four basic coaching principles. If we want to become aware of the programs that run us, we must practice coming back to this moment where we can begin to see what is there and what and who we are, *here*, in this moment.

In the same way that we look into mirrors to see reflections of our physical selves, it is possible to question what we see beyond the physical aspect. Physiologically, we are designed to not see our internal selves. It is possible though, for us to be aware of our limitations and be *here* with it all so we consciously have choices. To get there, I use the four main principles. I create my reality, and what I focus on expands into responsibility and action.

8 ◯ ∞

Homeplay

Read each question below. If you feel drawn to any of these questions, give yourself the gift of seeing the obstacles of your own dance.

1. Did you see yourself in any part of this chapter? If yes, which one? Can you trace it back to how you have learned this behavior and how or when it shows up today?
2. If you did not relate at all, what are your obstacles?

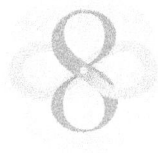

5

The Last Dance

*Learn to be quiet enough to hear
the genuine in yourself,
so that you can hear it in others.*

—Marian Wright Edelman

The *Selfprint*: A Unique Dance

Do you ever feel that there is no one else in the world like you? Our uniqueness, our *Selfprint*, is who we are before we misunderstood that we needed to be something else. You have probably heard this question, but it is worth repeating. What would you do if time or money were not an obstacle?

This is a great question to get us to take action. What about when we want to be more ourselves? Who are we before we learned we were also our obstacles—expectations, ideals, and perceptions of the person we think we should be? This question helps us expand our focus and see the possibilities that exist but are prevented from being seen by our conditioning. As children, we learn by copying others in our community. We must learn rules and social expectations to live in a community, but unconsciously, we internalize more than norms and expected behaviors. We incorporate standards and opinions of others into our self-perception. In psychoanalysis, internalization is part of the super-ego formation, the moralizing critical role. Internalization, although part of the original function of socialization—integration for survival—is what protects us, yet it also engulfs the self. Unless, however, the desired behaviors and rules we internalize from our primary caretakers reflect our own natural tendencies, we might believe we must be something else. Gradually, many of us stop coming into contact with what is true for ourselves. We become disconnected from who we are, and we reduce ourselves to follow others.

Part of mindfulness work, and the practice of embodied self-awareness, is the invitation to see who we are before we internalized who we ought to be. Edward Young, the early eighteenth-century British philosopher and poet, asked, "We are all born originals—why is it so many of us die copies?" Parents of identical twins know there are fundamental differences in each of their children, regardless of how much they look alike. Individual differences are clear at an early age. As bio-psycho-social beings, we are complex and simultaneously unique. Unfortunately, the complexity of our selves is not considered even with something as supposedly basic as gender.

Transgender people are probably the best at explaining this inner sense of self, or at least sensing what they are not. At the time of birth, children are assigned a label based only on the visible sex organ. There is no test done to understand the genetic expressions, neuroanatomical differences, or gene association with hormone receptors. Human biology is much more complex than the physical form it takes. There is a wide spectrum of possibilities between the binary of vaginas and penises. In reference to gender identity, the combinations are multiple.

Now, imagine all possibilities within this universe of a body that contains us. Our fingerprints confirm we are absolute originals both biologically and in the expression of our identities. Genetically we are 99.4 percent similar to any other human being.[20] Yet, our genetic code is so vast that the tiny percent left is enough to create important, distinct differences. Transgender people are clear on what they know they are not, perhaps because of the restrictive limiting binary form our societies see and use to label us. This is how our *Selfprint* works. Just because some of us identify as cisgender or gender wise, does not mean our true identity is how we were originally labeled. Our uniqueness is real and when ignored becomes a nagging sensation, a knock at our inner-self door. We must own our identity because our uniqueness is important information for our dance.

In my early days as a life coach, my role was to help people set and meet their goals, which I did, until one day I got an email from a client. Ann explained that her dream job was great and the pay was just what she had written on the goal-setting exercise we had developed. The position allowed for everything she had asked for: growth, a raise, and a respectful yet fun work environment. However,

Ann continued, "There is something missing." With great confusion and sadness, Ann was asking for my help to "get there" again, the new image of what would remove this sense of "something missing." Ann wanted to set another goal, an even bigger one to make this "old feeling" go away.

This episode with Ann made me realize that creating another goal would not make her happier. It would instead cause Ann to keep chasing something outside of herself. *Here*, we needed to turn toward this old feeling, get to know it well, listen to what it really needed as opposed to bargaining for what Ann imagined would get her out of this feeling. I asked Ann several questions first, out of my own need to understand what I had done wrong. If she had been successful in achieving the goal, there should be no problem, right? Wrong! In our sessions, I continued to make sure Ann's wants and needs were aligned. What came up was this image Ann had internalized of who she needed to be. She had been chasing this ideal self as opposed to honoring the person she was and is. Ann kept achieving goals, hoping that this imaginary life would make her something else, but this sensation kept "calling her." So, we played with the feelings and touched this sensation. First, we zoomed in to touch it and got to know it closely. We tried to understand what it was asking of Ann. Slowly and gently we gathered information about her beliefs, values, and needs. We zoomed in and got closer to hear the music already playing at a low volume inside her. Sometimes it was too much, so we would zoom out of all those details to see the wider picture, and from there, awareness grew. Together, we zoomed in and out at the unique rhythm of the dance. We danced with and between what arose.

The dance happens between the inner and outer world, the small and the wider, the self and the community.

The philosopher, author, and teacher, Ken Wilber, developed an integral model and in his book, *The Brief History of Everything* the author explains how and where each one fits in relation with all the others. The integral concept celebrates that everybody is an important piece is this push/pull, the dance between the individual and the collective, the internal and external world. There is a tangible and intangible, learned and not learned part of ourselves. How can we embrace that we are both this unique *Selfprint* and yet 99.4 percent the same as other human beings? We are unique and a collective beat breathing. We need both. Can we live in unity within paradoxes?

Each one of us has the choice to create our reality in each moment even though we live in this complex world that we do not control nor fully understand. It is our responsibility to be aware of the intersectionality of our lives and authentically create a meaningful life. Unless we are aware of our uniqueness, our efforts to create our reality are always going to be wasted. We are going to feel disconnected and exhausted. We then reinforce patterns of how we fight life, how we "prostitute" ourselves to meet our needs, and how we grow addicted to things that try to shush unpleasant feelings away. However, awareness gives us permission to be ourselves. We do not need to follow or control or even lead. We can live our truth, messy as it might be. We dance in our bodies the way we feel our own rhythm. When Ann unconsciously ignored her sense of self, she removed an essential part of herself from her dance. Is it possible to get to our essence without having to make all the mistakes of chasing what is not ours? My experience has led me to believe that "mistakes" are beneficial when we learn from them, but in this case, maybe we do not need that many to know the truth. Ann's *Selfprint* was showing her this old sensation, one that literally did not let her eat, a moving knot trying to untie itself. Ann had a checkup just to make sure it was nothing physical. She kept saying she felt something was missing in her life. The more Ann did and achieved, the tighter the knot inside her became, and the stronger the feeling was that she had to be somewhere else. With each goal she felt more resistance.

Our *Selfprint* is an energy, an inner calling in all of us, a voice begging us to listen, to notice, and to turn toward it. We dance our way through and become gently curious as we find the courage to dive into a new field. There is this something in us waiting for us to live it fully; it is patiently asking our attention to be manifested. Just as Ann mentioned, she felt this knot like it was calling out for her to notice. As she moved away the knot grew tighter, and when she moved toward it the knot loosened a little. Ann was using the sensation to guide her decisions and adjusted accordingly. Gradually Ann started spending more time in ways that reminded her of something familiar to her, an inner expression of who she is and had always been. Ann started taking time to be in nature and explore interests that she had always been curious about as a child. She even bought a telescope and started stargazing. The last time I saw Ann, she still loved her job, but she was in love with life. She started walking during her commute and listening to an audio course just for fun. Ann did not want to change jobs after all; she just needed to listen to her essence and live it a little more.

We often get distracted with the busyness of doing, meanwhile forgetting to live this expression of ourselves, the part of us that knows best. It also knows the universe and it does not die with our body. To find this true expression, we must listen to the pauses in the music playing and be present. There is an inner knowing of what matters, what is important, and what we must prioritize. All we need is to make space for us to touch it. I am passionate about inviting you to connect with your *Selfprint* and will use an exercise to guide your process. First, let us start at the beginning, or maybe, let us start at the end.

The Deathbed Exercise

Today, however, we are having
a hard time living because
we are so bent on outwitting death.

—SIMONE DE BEAUVOIR,
THE ETHICS OF AMBIGUITY

If you could choose, how would you like to feel about your life when you see yourself at your deathbed? It is crucial to wake up to who we are and know what matters in our lives. Otherwise, we may find ourselves in our deathbed with regrets and a sense of having wasted our lives. In my coaching training, I would always start with the end in mind. First, we must identify where we are, and then we can identify where we want to end up. Life coaches help clients create a vision, set a goal, define strategies, and figure out where we are heading. Then they develop consistent action steps to make sure we get there. Throughout the years, I realized that the goal, the "there" we say we want to get to, never delivers what we are truly seeking. Yes, we may get the job, the house, or the relationship, but generally we do not get what we most long for. Humans have many movable musical notes, and there is a uniqueness, an underlying beat.

My favorite way to listen for this inner beat is simple and pain free. People dislike its name; the *Deathbed Exercise*. Once a client agrees to work with me, our first session is an invitation to experience the Deathbed. Do not worry, the exercise is nothing like my first deathbed exercise out of Paulo Coelho's book, *The Pilgrimage*, the name alone is scary, the *Buried Alive Exercise*. The experience I had was so powerful that I was inspired to search for ways to create the same breakthrough effect without being morbid. The exercise I have developed is just an imaginary game where we relax and answer retrospective questions as if we were living the last hour of our lives. The exercise is about the life we lived, the lessons we learned, not about death itself. It shows us how alive mortality can be. Death has this force that allows us to shed all that is irrelevant. The greatest advantage of the *Deathbed Exercise* is its accessibility, its speedy effectiveness in getting us to a place of certainty. In front of death, we do not doubt what really matters the most for us.[21] We all know without doubt that all living things die. If it has a body, it will die. If nothing else, death is our common denominator. Regardless of physical or emotional characteristics, gender, race, sexual orientation, or religion, we all know we are going to die. It is this certainty that shakes us to our core, leaving only what really matters to us.

When we lack this certainty, we fail to set goals for our lives. People often say they want goals that they are either unsure about or are uncertain they can achieve. Without certainty, there is less drive. My role with a client is to explore that sense of certainty and start with the end in mind. The only end we agree with is the end in this body. Since the *Deathbed Exercise* is imaginary, clients let me know who they are and how their dance looks. They allow the imagination to flow without obstacles. At the last minute, dancing with the certainty of this last breath wakes us up to honor who we are and what it means to be alive. Research shows that people get clarity when they experience a nearly fatal accident, receive a diagnosis of a life-threatening disease, face the death of a loved one, or experience a drastic identity-changing event. When these events happen, people report a sudden shift as if they unexpectedly remembered what matters, who they truly are, and what they want. In her book, *The Top Five Regrets of the Dying*, author and live-in caretaker for terminal patients, Bronnie Ware, describes the anguish of those who, in their real final days, asked her to pass on messages so others would not make the same mistakes: the sense that their lives had something for them that they did not listen to. The idea of the *Deathbed Exercise is* to bring this inner knowing to the surface and shake it, to bring it back to life as it is often dormant. The hope is that, because the exercise is imaginary, you will drop your internalized defenses of what is possible, allowed, and not allowed. The goal is to acknowledge what matters most in a less painful way than we normally experience it during life-threatening wake up calls.

In his mid-30s, Alex was starting to feel bad about his life but did not understand why. He was also starting to have some health issues that he attributed to stress from his extremely demanding job. Hesitantly, he kept saying, "This is not me. This cannot be my life. I've worked hard to get all that I have, and I am proud of it but..." He was comfortable with what he had achieved. He had a good career in the education system, possibilities of a promotion and a raise, made relatively good money, and had a stable, loving relationship. Yet Alex was confused about why getting there was making him feel less of everything. He had a good life by everyone's standards. He kept telling me that he traveled, had a good family and good friends, but nonetheless, the sensations kept coming.

At this time, I was not yet using the *Deathbed Exercise* with every client. Having previously achieved great results with the exercise, I explained that what I was suggesting was a bit unconventional. Alex was open to engaging with the exercise. He ended the *Deathbed Exercise* with a clear image of himself at a very old age. He was able to touch a feeling of accomplishment and a living of a life with purpose, service, contribution, and laughter. Alex felt this was what he wanted to feel about his life and what he wanted to tell his grandchildren about his life. In essence, this was precisely what Alex wanted to feel every day. He felt speechless, but he described a lightness in his chest, an exciting yet calm sense about his life, and a smile in his heart. Even though he saw he would face inevitable difficulties like the death of his parents, Alex knew he would get through it fully. He felt alive and eager to bring these found sensations into his everyday life. By the next session, Alex had already developed a new goal. He researched what he needed for this transition, and he knew he had to try. Alex shared that the sensations he experienced during the exercise kept recurring, and this scared him. However, he was willing to take a risk. Alex decided to postpone his engagement. He was going to ask for a loan and go back to school while still working. It was not going to be easy, but he had touched his *Selfprint* and seen what he needed to do. Alex told me he could not afford to work with me anymore but asked me if he could occasionally email. I welcomed his news.

A year later, I got an email from Alex saying he had never felt so alive. He did not have much time or money but was in love with his old man (the older version of himself in his Deathbed) who was helping him every step of the way. He also shared some hardships and obstacles that were in the way. It was difficult for some family members and a few old friends to understand what Alex was doing, but he had also found some support. Money was at center stage as he was still paying his student loans. Mainly, Alex was aware that even the hardships were part of a complex flowing dance that is both challenging and fulfilling. Two years later, I received an email announcing his graduation and scheduled interviews with non-profit organizations he admired. Last year, I got an email from Alex thanking me. He shared that in retrospect he sees he was numbly heading into a crash.

It is not always easy to know who we are and live our own truth, but when we do, it is a game changer. This peculiar exercise allows us to feel both mortal and alive, and at the same time it invariably stirs up our awareness. This distinctive moment of insight provides a standpoint from which we can look over our life as uniquely precious and decide how to dance with it. The apparent opposites are there to charge us with the wholeness of our existence. *Here*, our mortality may remind us to fully live our *Selfprint*. This can leave us feeling alive when we take our last breath. What would it take for you to be at your deathbed feeling what you would like to feel?

My Hospital Deathbed Exercise

People living deeply have no fear of death.

—ANAïS NIN

I have been inviting clients to play with an imaginary *Deathbed Exercise*, to connect with their inner truths, and shed what is not relevant so they can consciously be the life they dance. This exercise is part of my everyday calendar. Oddly, it never crossed my mind that one day I would find myself going through the experience, but for real.

I am burning in fever and half asleep when a doctor tells me I have to be placed in isolation. I am confused and afraid of the approaching diagnosis. The contagious infection unit is on the top floor of the highest building in town. I have the best views, and I am grateful for that. The head doctor comes in and tells me that my immunity is severely low. I thank him for the information. He looks puzzled. "I'm not sure you understand the gravity of your condition," he says. "You can die!" He said this as if this piece of information was saved for last resorts only. "You can die!" What if this is my last hour? I smile, as I remembered that this could be my real deathbed. I stare at the beautiful view and feel this immense peace, a calm certainty that I could die. There is a certain curiosity, even excitement, as I have flashbacks of my life: holding my baby sister for the first time, riding my bicycle, having my first bedroom just for myself, touching my older sister's belly and feeling the baby kick, meeting my new born niece, eating melted ice cream on my first date, holding my nephew's little hand, having my niece meet me at the airport, missing my family and friends, failing at so much, achieving so much, feeling lost, loving so many important people, the dry mountain dessert, the sunrises, the ocean, so many different places. Sometimes life is a mess, sometimes it is magic, and sometimes it is everything in between. I lived it all and a lot of it in the uniqueness of my weird being. I also sold myself. I fought. I resisted. I served. I loved. I laughed. I danced. And most importantly, I learned to follow my own beat.

I had to ask myself, "If this is my last hour alive, what do I want to feel about my life?" The answer was clear: this is it.

I am at my most peaceful ever. I am vibrating. I stare out the window and a thought steals my attention. I see my mother and sisters' grief as if it was a rock hitting me. Honestly, I am intrigued. I was not expecting this. I stay with it for a little bit, but it is too much for me. I force myself to remember the first sensations when I felt the peaceful, calm energy. So I move back and forth, holding these two real experiences in my weak body, bringing them both closer to me because they are so beautiful. What I am feeling is life, my whole life. Feeling others' pain is also life. It is part of the beauty of being alive, of having lived fully, of having made a difference and touched hearts with who I am. The polar opposite sensations of peace and pain, *here*, in my heart, remind me that my life has been an entire dance and that it mattered. I am grateful for life, inside and outside. The *Deathbed Exercise* I guided so many people through taught me to be in this hospital bed. I just hope to feel that gratitude and awe about my life every single day I am alive.

The imaginary *Deathbed Exercise* is this simple invitation. It serves as a reminder that I create my reality in each moment, we all do. When I consider my unique *Selfprint*, I am reminded to claim my inner power and to make choices, in this moment, that reflect how I want to live. This exercise can be a wakeup call. Living with mortality is accepting to be humble in all my power. If I die feeling this much love, this peace, this energy, I am sure I will die happy to have created my reality and danced this life in my own messy way. This is what I wish for my clients and you, my readers. I wish that we can deeply live in the awareness *here*, as our most authentic selves, respecting our uniqueness as an integral part of the whole. May we awaken to this dance. Until then, we must first practice giving voice to our inner music.

8   ○   ∞

Homeplay

Dive into what is most alive in you and choose to play with these questions.

1. What is your experience of yourself? What is unique about you?
2. Have you had a moment, an event, or a sudden change that made you forget the busyness of your life? Did that change give you information about what matters the most to you?
3. What if you lived from this knowing, this meaning of being alive? What would you do more of? What would you do less of? Who would you connect with?

6

Turning Into Your Inner Music

We are the local embodiment of a Cosmos grown to self-awareness. We have begun to contemplate our origins: starstuff pondering the stars; organized assemblages of ten billion billion billion atoms considering the evolution of atoms; tracing the long journey by which, here at least, consciousness arose.

—CARL SAGAN

Earphones Off—Tune Into Your Inner Song

Have you ever noticed something calling you from inside? According to Astronomer, Astrophysicist, and Poet, Carl

Sagan, we are the embodiment of a cosmos grown into self-awareness. Our inner song is rich and diverse, so amazingly complex, we might not always know its tune. Still, we all know when we are not tuned into our truth. It feels like being in an abusive relationship where we walk on eggshells to preserve an imagined future. We avoid conflicts; however, we cannot avoid the unavoidable. We abuse ourselves when we try to please another who can never be pleased. We disconnect from our inner richness and keep trying one more thing, one other adjustment. I used to work with violence against women issues, and I could not understand why women returned to their abusers, until I saw the program running in myself. Victims of violence do not stay because they like to be used and abused. They stay when they are not connecting with their own truth.

Ruth arrived for her session visibly disturbed. I noticed she had no makeup on, which was unusual. Her eyes glared as though she had been crying, which she confirmed. Ruth had a fight with her partner. They exchanged insults. He had pushed her and told her to leave. She was feeling sad, angry, confused, and mostly lost. This relationship was her focus, her dream. Ruth was planning the wedding, not this! She told me a little about what happened and then described his addiction, his inability to admit it, and his unwillingness to fix it. She was disillusioned. I listened for a bit and asked Ruth where she was placing her focus. She stopped, sensing where I was heading. She replied, "On him." We spoke about the reality Ruth was creating. The more Ruth described what she wanted, the easier it was for her to shift her focus. Her breathing slowed down, her eyes became a bit brighter, more open, and there was a smile on the corner of her mouth. Directing her focus to two questions—who

Ruth was and what she wanted for her life—was enough for Ruth to remember who she was and how powerful she could be, even with this emotional pain. We focused on what Ruth wanted and were decisive in goal setting.

We are told to focus on what we want in order to manifest it. We must know our weaknesses and strengths. We design a goal using the SMART five golden rules, or the 12 steps to goal setting. We even have a clear vision. Our goal is specific and measurable. It has a time frame and is achievable and relevant. We can build it into action steps, and we are motivated. My question is, if we can all reach goals, why are we not happier in our experience of life? We get the results, most of the time we even get our designed dream goal, the job, or the relationship. We get there, we celebrate, and we are happy—for a brief moment at least. However, this is a disillusion. The ball keeps moving and we create another goal.

When we focus on our goals, it is like focusing on moving targets. We keep having to create another goal, and we are never satisfied because we are searching for a goal to give us the wrong thing. We already are everything we need. We can get there by being *here*, by being who we are. Wait, hear me out, my experience tells me this happens with so many of us. We have achieved goals. We have worked hard for a degree, a relationship, wealth, health, or a fitness goal and what happened? I am not saying that we should not work for the things we want. Goals are important and we can have them. My goal right now is to finish this book. What I am saying is we must remember to turn the focus to our Self first, play with it and see it in our lives, test it out at our own rhythm. Getting to my goal, having this book published will not make me anything that I am not already. It will give me an experience I did not have and knowledge of this process, and it will solidify who I am when facing the difficulties in each step. But finishing this book will not add value to who I am. Unless I keep noticing my Self, unless I am *here* with everything that is happening in me, this book will just be another task on my to-do list. As I am writing, I notice that achieving this goal will be fun. It will give me a sense of accomplishment, but it will not add or remove from who I already AM. Regardless of what will happen, I will not be more nor will I be less.

Western cultures believe that achievements make us more. This idea trained me to focus on something outside of myself to be happy. Focus is an important ability in life and is the skill to turn our undivided attention to one thing. Focus is also needed to sustain our ability to create our reality *here*, to be in our power with what is. We know this, yet there is something preventing us from directing our focus toward what makes a difference. Unless we know where to focus, we will be led by anything that moves outside of ourselves. We believe the music comes only from the outside.

We resist taking our earphones off because of two major beliefs. First, in the western world at least, we are conditioned to chase something outside of ourselves. This is rewarded and reinforced socially with celebrations of milestones such as graduating, getting a job or a promotion, buying a house or a car, or getting married. Second, there is a series of religious and philosophical teachings that cast a bad spell on turning to the self. The Bible and the Qur'an have references that turning inward makes us selfish. "Let no one seek his own good, but that of his neighbor" (1 Corinthians 10:24). "Allah does not love anyone vain or boastful" (Qur'an, 4:36). Buddhism sees the self as the source of suffering. Western society is suffering greatly with selfishness nowadays. This includes the inability to consider the impact that our actions have on others, the use and abuse of power, manipulation of the masses with complete disregard of its impact, toleration of disrespect, lack of willingness to put ourselves in someone else's struggles, and many other widespread selfish attitudes.

I know I am only selfish when I am unaware of my inner truth, when I am unable to be embodied *here*. When I am scared, I become blind even to my values and beliefs. I also see this over and over with other people, including my clients. We act irrationally and are inconsiderate when we do not know ourselves inside, when we do not know our natural, complex, rich world of sensations, emotions, feelings, and thoughts. This is when we are selfish and childlike. It is appropriate for children to not have these abilities, but as adults it is fundamental that we learn to know our inner world. If I cannot notice, identify, and name my own fear, I cannot notice someone else's. The other is acting on his fear, and I am reacting on mine. There is no communication possible. There is only fighting and arguing. Because I learned to overvalue what comes from outside, I did not develop the ability to care for my inner world. I got stuck in this vicious cycle. Until I started developing this inner, deeper self-awareness, I was not capable of seeing the other as subjects in their own right. If we do not turn inward and get to know our Selves, we will continue to see others as objects that we use at will, and that is selfish indeed. Although unconscious, it is contagious and sickening, and we are seeing this in our current world. Embodied self-awareness can change this.

This practice can bring clarity to the difference between being completely self-absorbed and being able to notice our inner world. This distinction is important, and it gives us space to explore our inner experiences without being afraid of turning selfish. In defense of those who are self-absorbed, we must recognize that this often starts in infancy. Children who are not helped to understand their own sensations and emotions are unable to experience and integrate them. Such a child develops selfish behavior as a defense mechanism, a protective attempt to cope. The more the child learns to use behaviors, things, and people at his disposal to disconnect from the inner discomfort, the less empathy he will likely learn. Taken to an extreme, this behavior can become a diagnosed pathology. No wonder people are afraid of turning inside. But embodied self-awareness is actually the antidote. So, if we want to be considerate, kind, and thoughtful, please practice being *here* and turn to the inner world. This single act of turning inward can stop arguments and prevent wars. Do not take my word for it, experiment with it. Let us take our earphones off and tune in. Let us notice the complexity of our music and experience the difference it can bring.

By focusing on oneself, we can assess where we are, what is happening within us, and what is possible for us in these circumstances now. Inside, we have all our belief systems, values, opinions, judgements, feelings, and emotions, along with every sensation in the body. This is the reason I start turning inward. I zoom in to come closer and see in detail. If I want something of life, I first start within, then I zoom out to gain perspective and see how the details are needed for understanding. From a more distant perspective, while still focusing on this moment, I also see the messages from our culture asking us to do the exact opposite, to turn to the outside, to "keep our eyes on the ball and go get it." Being *here* shows that we are the ball to which we need to turn our attention.

So, when during her session Ruth started focusing on her partner and wanting him to do something different, be someone different, I asked her where she was focusing. Even if her partner could be different, even if he would, what made the biggest difference for Ruth was to start focusing on what was happening inside herself first. From there, Ruth remembered. Ruth reconnected with what was happening for her and could see what was really important. When she zoomed in to the moment and turned to her emotions, she could see it.

Being *here* gives Ruth access to her information. In awareness of her inner world with her needs and wants, she can zoom out and start to notice herself in relation to the roles she plays. She can see the other people and the roles they play. She can see things in time and space and have a choice. Embracing her truth, she also knew what was possible. Ruth knows it can be fun to get what she wants outside, but what she really wants is something her partner cannot give her. She becomes more able to recognize what she can and cannot hold in this moment. Ruth is aware that her inner experience is what is creating her reality and her focus is just reinforcing it. As soon as Ruth takes her earphones off and tunes into her inner song, her truth, she also touches her own inner power to dance life by showing up in the moment.

Reclaiming Our Inner Power

What are you really capable of? I am aware of social and structural inequalities in our world and how these facilitate or limit possibilities for each one of us. The power I am referring to in this section is an inner power, not outer power. This inner power is what I believe allows so many to overcome the most adverse circumstances. This power reminds us that as human beings, no matter what, we are all born equal.

As I touched my *Selfprint*, this part that is beyond what I had learned to be, I started reclaiming my power. When we do this, we become able to act in alignment with the embodied experience of ourselves. Inner power, in the context of this practice of reclaiming our power, is using our unique energy and acting effectively. Unfortunately, power as a social construct is perceived as force or power over something or another, and this is not what inner power is. It is living and dancing our own spark. Our inner power is already available, regardless of circumstances. Let us use it because it has been *here* since we were born and exists for our benefit and the good of all. Having said this, reclaiming my power is semantically incorrect, as I cannot reclaim what was never not mine. In our rushed existence, we hide behind the roles we play and forget how to live by our power.

When I first met Maggie, I was impressed by her brighter-than-life smile. This young woman, full of dreams, desperately wanted to do something that would contribute to a better world. Maggie had finished her master's degree, and although young, she already had vast experience in her field. In her country, however, there were not many job opportunities in her field. Money was short, and Maggie had just moved in with friends when she asked for my help. Her focus was on her circumstances. She blamed herself and felt bad about her situation. We started working on the four basic principles, and I kept asking Maggie to notice how she was creating her reality—not the unemployment, not the lack of money, not her housing circumstances, but who she was and is. Little by little Maggie started touching that part of herself that she remembered. First, it was a memory of a moment playing in an open field, then an experience at her grandmother's house, then a recurring sensation. Even her laughter shifted.

Maggie was remembering who she was and is. The more she touched her *Selfprint*, the more she could access her true nature.

As much as Maggie loved the sessions and the *Homeplays* to dive deeper, she could not stop worrying about her future. She would sit for hours in front of a computer applying for jobs and ended up surfing the web. At the end of the day, Maggie would feel unproductive and blamed herself for doing nothing. I asked Maggie to set a date for herself. If by then nothing had shifted for her, she would get to her plan B and immigrate again. Maggie agreed. The more she allowed herself to play with what was coming up in her inner world, the more she started making different choices, and step by step, she created a different reality. For example, initially Maggie thought she could not have fun until she had a job, but the more Maggie chose to enjoy her day, the easier it was to remember to focus on what she could do in the moment. Maggie allowed herself to enjoy planning and cooking more nutritious meals. She would go for long walks in the fields and started an exercise routine. Maggie was even engaging with others she met at her bus stop. Each week, Maggie would report some new breath of fresh air in her life. She started getting more interviews. Maggie took on part-time jobs that had nothing to do with what she wanted, but Maggie knew that it was the way she was choosing to live this period in her life that was creating her reality. So, she did not identify with what she was doing in her work at a call center. She took it as a learning experience, a way to have some pocket money and meet new people.

As I share Maggie's story, I cannot stop smiling. It brought joy to my heart seeing how much Maggie claimed her power. Her smile got even brighter. Maggie felt overwhelmed with her circumstances and thinking about the future was weighing her down. As she turned away from the outside world, the facts, and the "doing," and connected with her truth, Maggie remembered who she already was. Before, she thought that her value came from her paycheck or title. All Maggie needed was to shift her old beliefs and spend time with herself. The more Maggie turned into her truth, the more it was possible for her to act in accordance and live her *Selfprint*. She reclaimed her power by making choices that reflected what is unique about her.

As Maggie's situation revealed, her power was not what she had or did. It was not material possessions, not even achievements and trophies. This power is so much more than how much we do or even what we do. The more Maggie lived the expression of those sensations and memories of who she is, her own way, the more powerful she felt. When we reconnect with our inner power, we access a guiding compass, and this is what the world needs of us. I love when clients complain about a situation in one session and in the next session report that they cannot really explain what happened. Placed in the same situation, they felt this power, an inner knowing that had their backs. In that moment, they could be respectful and calm yet firm and determined. Once, a client who had to face an important meeting told me, "I don't know where this came from, but I just stood up and felt stronger than I had ever been. I said what I had to say, standing my ground." These are just a few of the moments I love to witness in my clients and their willingness to dance.

It is important to remember these realizations are not constant. In fact, nothing in a dance is constant. There are changes, and sometimes during different phases in life we need to forget ourselves to play a role. With mothers of newborns and in certain professions, there are moments when we must fulfill a certain role. For example, we do not want a mother to say, "Now I need to sleep so I can't feed my baby." Nature is well designed. This power reminds us that we are not the roles we play, important as they might be. We are dancing between playing the roles and forgetting our true nature. When, as we do, we get completely embedded in a role, life gently pulls this role away as if to say, "See, you are not the role you were playing. You are still *here*." When I get these reminders, and only after kicking and screaming first, I remember. Even if only for a brief moment, I remember who I really am, until I find myself embedded in yet another role. Sometimes these roles I play are real. I am a sister, a friend, a professional. Other times the roles I play are stories of identity. I am the one who knows stuff, I am the one who helps others, or I am the one who always replies to emails on time. From *here* I can see life smiling and playing along in this remembering-and-forgetting sacred dance.

Today, Maggie is well employed and working for an organization aligned with her life values. She has a position that reflects her level of education and her skills. Maggie is also learning a great deal about a new system in a different setting. She is working in service of others as she wanted. Above all, Maggie is making a difference while earning the kind of money that allows her to pay her student loans and plan for her future. Maggie is valuing her work and herself, and she is also feeling valued by those for whom she works. Sometimes work demands long hours, but it is all part of the dance. Every now and then I get a message or comment on social media from Maggie, thanking me for the gems she still uses in her daily life. I am glad Maggie noticed what was creating her reality and made small changes to reclaim her power and use her energy to dance life. Remembering and forgetting who we are is stronger during transitions. When the roles we play disappear, we tend to forget that who we are does not come from these roles. Forgetting our real identity makes us want to hold on to the perceived identities these roles provide. I did the exact same thing when I moved to the US and could not work; I forgot who I was and felt a sense of lost identity. Even worse, I attached myself to the identity of the useless one. I forgot then, as I forget often, who I truly am. Once I remember, it does not matter what I do as long I remember my inherent value. Have you been through a divorce, a loss of a job, or a debilitating injury? During these transitions it can be challenging to remember who we truly are.

My personal and professional experience has shown me that transitions can be hard. We want to be the DJs of life. We want to control the songs and their sequences, and so we fight the transitions. However, the more we allow these transitions to be opportunities for us to reconnect and remember, the more we touch this inner gentle power. Just like with Maggie, the more she allowed her *Selfprint* to live through her actions, the more she aligned, the more she had to contribute to the world. By turning to her inner power, she danced. I believe that our true expression is what the world needs most from us, like with Maggie. As the saying goes, "Be the change we want to see in the world."

8   ○   ∞

Homeplay

How playful can you get with this? If an embodied experi-ence can bring us back to the wisdom of the cosmos, how can we reconnect with it all?

1. If you were to turn your earphones off and turn inside, what would you find? Easy and simple sensations, move-ment, vibration, temperature, form, etc.
2. How do you define power? Who do you consider power-ful? How much of this is power and how much is force—or power over?
3. What if power was not what most of us learn it is?

7

Rewrite Your Moves

There is no greater agony than bearing an
untold story inside you.

—MAYA ANGELOU,
I KNOW WHY THE CAGED BIRD SINGS

Knowing the Program Running Us

Can you identify the influences of your thinking, the triggers of your emotions, and the urges of your body? I need to remind myself over and over again that this is a dance that comes and goes. The practice of being *here* has given me some ability to notice what ideas come from the outside environment and what comes from my internal compass.

Outside influences include countries of origin, religion, politics, education, and language. We should be taught how to tell the difference when we are young, but most of us do not learn to turn to ourselves and notice the richness of our inner world. What we internalize is the opposite. We are taught to believe that who we are is wrong and that we need to be more like the images we see. From my family I learned I had to be a well-behaved, quiet girl. Then in school I learned not to ask questions and always have the right answer. Then media showed me what kind of a woman I should aspire to be. As a mixed-race girl growing up in a coffee plantation, I did not look like the images of women in magazines. They were tall and thin and had long blond hair, blue eyes, perfect bodies, and perfect teeth. I operated under this program without being conscious of it. This practice, this curiosity in knowing who I am as a whole, keeps saving my life.

I once worked with an integrative medical clinic that used a comprehensive approach to health and wellbeing. We were a diverse professional team working collaboratively to support each client. One day, I was asked by one of our doctors to speak with her patient. Her name was Di, and she was a young woman who had come to the clinic because of chronic pain. I introduced myself and my role at the clinic, but Di did not seem interested. I was curious, so I gave her my card and asked if I could email her. I emailed her asking how she was doing, and Di politely replied with just the lyrics of a song. That said it all—she was carrying too much on her shoulders. Months went by before Di showed up on my calendar for a session. I was very curious to know what brought her back.

In our session, Di explained that she was tired of being in pain as a result of a childhood injury that was worsened by a series of medical procedures. Di shared that no one could help her, but I had said something that had intrigued her. In my introduction I had said, without knowing anything about her, that I knew she was not what she had been told she was. There was a program running her and that program was the main cause of her suffering, even more so than her pain. Although true, I do not always tell my clients in an intro session that the program running us causes more suffering than any pain could possibly cause. My intention was not to diminish Di's chronic pain but to acknowledge both the tangible and intangible as painfully real. Physical pain needs a certain type of approach and so does the program that is running us.

Consciousness Always Includes

The programs that run us can be more debilitating than any physical pain. Emotionally, we inherit these programs that run us in similar ways as we inherit our DNA. What we do not inherit before we were born; we absorb unconsciously, at a young age. These programs are essential acculturation tools that prepare us to live in communities. It is as if our parents and society have handed us the only song they knew how to sing. Regardless of possibly being the best we could have inherited, these programs fail our nature. They prevent us from seeing beyond the obvious. Awareness and practice allow us to distinguish these running programs. We may even learn to use the program for our benefit and update our software. Imagine that one day we leave our small village and hear music on the radio and then learn to read music and start composing. It may not be complicated, but it is also not a one-stop quick fix either.

Let me be clear here; I am not referring to self-programming as a way to control, manipulate, or modify ourselves to become something or someone else. I am not saying we need to be more or better. These codes are already running through us. Tons of those kinds of programs are already available, such as "7 days to become a better you," "30 daily tips to self-improvement," and "21 strategies to a better you this year." Many vow to transform us into improved versions of ourselves. These programs can be effective for specific situations such as learning a new skill. I am all for learning and growing and am glad neuroplasticity has proven that old dogs can learn new tricks. Nevertheless, the "how to get out of here and get there" kind of program does not deliver what I long for. Quick fixes are behavioral changes, which despite being important, do not promote embodied living. The emphasis *here* is being in consciousness, not transformation; not doing, but being. Are you a human who is doing?

These are the first steps of what I call self-programming for consciousness. This huge task of seeing what is seeing. It is practically the opposite of what the self-help industry promotes. Consciousness starts with pausing, being, stillness, allowing what is, and seeing all that life carries. It is this simple non-doing step that creates room for all other changes to take place. The acceptance and the recognition of the old programs allow the program to run while I am present with it. This does not remove the program; it is non-action that shifts so much. Without revealing much about her life, and without believing this practice would be helpful, Di was curious enough to allow herself to play with it. Little by little, Di turned to her program and what she had learned when she was a child. What had she absorbed about how to deal with pain? Di became aware of her belief system in relation-ship to pain. Specifically, regarding what pain meant about her. How much of her identity became wrapped around her condition? How much of herself was diminished because of her situation? Noticing what was there, Di ventured out to do things differently. For example, she waited a few sec-onds before taking her medication to notice what meanings she was giving to taking or not taking medication. She just noticed with curiosity and kindness. By noticing the mean-ings she gave to her body and pain, Di also experienced new sensations.

It is not easy to turn the eye to our own programming and see the ocean in which we swim. Seeing beyond the obvi-ous of what we have been trained to see requires audacity and willingness. Funnily, this practice requires us to turn to the body, learn its language, and investigate our emotions.[22] We must get to know our emotions closely and learn their unique language. We can include our personal histories, our made-up stories, as well as those of our ancestors. Epigenetics claims our ancestors' stories can influence our choices and behaviors even when we are not consciously aware of what was passed on to us. Our work is to turn to it, see it, and get to know how it operates. It can be helpful to have someone else supporting us when we learn anything new. Di contin-ued allowing herself to dance with what was hers without trying to change anything, not even her pain. Of course, she had always wanted to change the pain, but now she realized the distinction. To address the physical pain, she used acu-puncture, specific massages, physiotherapy, and medication. The practice we developed required her to become aware of the programs running her without her awareness and permis-sion. This program was limiting her dance moves more than if she had no legs or arms. She quickly understood that this was a practice she would hold on to for years to come.

Self-programming for consciousness is the never-ending endeavor to see ourselves as an intricate part of this universe, in constant change and highly connected to everything. This interconnectedness is not pre-deterministic and is a condition that needs our awareness. This is what happens inside us when we hear a song. It is what makes us move. It is not the song alone, but a blend of what happens inside of us when it gets touched by the song. How many little things happen? Body sensations, emotions, memories, old experiences, thoughts, feelings—all of this happens and creates the movement from within. We will not fully know it or understand it all, but it is fundamental that we turn toward this with the intention of recognizing it, to see it for what it is. Due to its complexity, the turning-toward practice cannot be prescribed. It is a simple invitation to be curious and present. Of course, it is never complete. It is a practice of being *here*. It is the awareness of us as subjects, not as objects; of us as alive agents with rich, fully lived inner experiences; human beings in constant change in the vastness of this universe who also have a whole lot of programs running and learned schemas. The past is an integral part of our experience, but it does not need to dictate our future.

Seeing Past Influences

Each experience and meaning given reinforces the preexisting program. Unless we remain conscious of our thoughts, each single thought is just keeping us where we have been. It is said that 90 percent of our thoughts are recurrent thoughts based on past experiences. The patterns become sustainable, and instead of having conscious awareness of them, we become results of the unconscious programs running us in a repetitive loop. This is not all bad. Our reflex and automatic nature facilitates tasks so we do not have to think about every detail. We do not need to make the heart pump or contract the muscles to digest food. Luckily, these things are done for us. Our autonomic nervous systems are sophisticated and intelligent, but they nevertheless require us to be watchful. Disease is triggered when we disregard our body's rhythms and signals. We know what our thoughts do on their own when we are not in the body. Living in autopilot prevents growth, creativity, and learning. It prevents us from expanding and from truly touching the multiple possibilities that are already *here*. That is why this takes practice.

The present moment demands our attention. It is said that what we repeatedly think, we create. Our brain is a complex, dynamic center of billions of signals sent from neuron to neuron in different regions of the brain. Neural pathways are the paths formed by the passing along of electrochemical messages. The higher the number and the intensity of the signals, the stronger the pathway. Repetition reinforces a habit, making it easier to be disengaged while thinking or doing something else. The Human Brain Project is a large-scale, collaborative scientific research project for the advancement of understanding the brain. The project combines neuroscience, computing, and brain-related medicine. It recognizes the complexity of the multiple systems' networks and the impact these have on consciousness and disorders of consciousness. The brain changes the way we live, and where we live and what we do changes its patterns. Hence the importance of practicing being *here*. Can we notice what is running in automatic mode? I sometimes catch myself in the kitchen with something in my hand, or literally in my mouth, that I did not consciously choose to eat. It is as if my eyes see a piece of fruit or some seeds, and a fast automatic signal reaches my brain, moving me to eat it. The program reinforces itself, and our habits turn into addictions. I know I am not alone in these automatic habits. My lack of awareness is the first step to shifting into a conscious decision-making process.

Embodied self-awareness opens space for the automatic to be noticed. Where else in my life am I *not* choosing rationally? Where else am I choosing what is familiar and effortless for my brain pathways? As humans we are products of our confirmation bias, which is a natural tendency to look for information that reinforces our own preexisting beliefs or experiences. "What we see is all there is" is how Daniel Kahneman,[23] the 2002 Nobel Prize winner in Economic Sciences and a psychologist known for his work in judgement and decision making, explains our inherited programs. Whatever happens, we only read it according to what we already have in us. We are incapable of seeing beyond that. We delete or distort facts to fit into our existing program. Since the program is running on what it knows, its previous experience, we continue to reproduce more of what was there before. Practicing presence is even more relevant when we want to change a habit, a diet, or learn a foreign language. It takes more than a conscious decision to change a behavior because change requires practice to become aware of the mechanisms and its variables already in place. For example, when I am aware of my inner state, I notice the slight distinctions as I enter the kitchen and when I look at the fruit. I do not change anything, but I notice the quick shifts in me wanting to eat. If I am present, I can consciously choose to eat or not. The system works for itself, and the more I practice being *here* the more able I become of choosing consciously. This is what Di has been dancing with in her experience.

Through small steps, Di started noticing, seeing, and realizing she was living under the spell of her programming. She believed her repetitive ideas that if she was in pain, she was not enough. She believed that she was not worthy of having what others had. Di saw how this conditioned the way she saw her future. She stopped believing and she stopped planning for it. Di had stopped engaging with what she loved, and she was continuously frightened. As Di noticed how her program was shrinking her and telling her lies, she saw the ideas running constantly, interfering with little tasks and decisions. She felt cursed and excluded of possibilities. Di was carrying a lot on her shoulders. Once she noticed the weight was from her program, she realized she could consciously change her moves. Her curiosity led her to play and be able to be with her fear for a few seconds. As she listened to her fear of the pain, of not being able to be functional and work, of not being independent, she gained courage. The more she noticed her own fear, the easier it was for Di to choose the moves doable in each moment. Slowly, Di started rewriting her moves. She persistently paid attention to what was possible in the moment. Di heard the same music but chose to move differently. Di started with what was present and explored what was possible, *here.*

When Di furthered her self-inquiry, she noticed her inner dialogue, the constant chattering that she carried. She also started noticing that these voices were not all hers. She carried the load of her doctors' opinions, of the schoolkids who bullied her. Di learned to be with her body's old program, to identify the learned reactions. She distinguished the requests for distractions to alleviate not the pain, but the emotional suffering. Di overate to cope. Her childhood chocolate chip cookies seemed to provide her some release. The old habit turned into addiction that brought more beliefs about her unworthiness. She can now hear these beliefs being spelled out and hear them asking for more cookies. The behaviors are reactions to alleviate the unbearable emotions that she carries on her shoulders. When Di sees her mind wanting to control, she now turns to her body and listens to all the information, noticing what is possible.

To this day, Di continues her practices and continues to become the agent of her life. The acceptance is inclusive. Yes, Di also fights what is when the pain is too intense, but now, in awareness, Di sees herself fighting. Di writes to me to share how she smiles when she recognizes her old program. Now she does not reject what is *here*, she sees it. When possible, she holds what the old urges ask for. The old song does not sound the same anymore, and even the song is starting to become more like a remix with a different beat. Di is now living independently. She has returned to college to study one of her passions. Di does not let her past dictate her future. She also dreams of sharing what she has learned to help others. This new remix is allowing Di to choose the moves for her dance while respecting her own rhythm.

Self-programming for consciousness is not a goal; it is a dance that is neither static nor final. The songs keep being rewritten, different moves appear according to possibilities, and the dance keeps flowing. The dance allows pain and program to co-exist. A dance does not exclude, nor does it want it to end. Instead, it happens in each moment. Beyond the obvious, Di dances with it all as she keeps rewriting her program with what she sees happening. Never over, it is a dance, and it can restart at any time. This is life, the dance of being here, as she is, as things are in the moment. It takes practice, but it can change everything.

8 ◯ ∞

Homeplay

If you choose to accept this invitation:

1. Identify a belief that you have about yourself. I am...
2. What influenced you to believe this about yourself?
3. When is this not true?
4. How do you feel about just noticing the belief and noticing when it is not true?

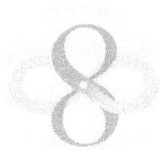

8

Dance Practice

*An ounce of practice is worth
more than tons of preaching.*

—Mahatma Gandhi

Practice, Practice, Practice!

Are you open to create a beginner's attitude? Although it is impossible to rehearse a choreography for life, we can practice the basic steps, surrender to the music, and flow. I grew up dancing and I love to dance. The last time I tried to learn specific dance moves was with a Brazilian friend who was teaching me his traditional *Forró* Dance. I have a video where you can hear Sofia, his wife, saying in Portuguese, *"Entregou"* ("she surrendered"). While I was trying to learn just the steps, I was too much in my head. I was too worried about doing the moves correctly. Once I surrendered to the beat and let myself be guided, it all came together. First, I practiced the basic steps. The practice allowed me to surrender to the music. In life, the basic steps are this exercise of *being here*. Once we are present, we can flow with life. Being alive is not always pretty or fun. At the beginning of the book, I shared my story to highlight that I too know loss, death, change, and hardships. This practice has literally saved my life as well as saving my sanity and well-being.

It is easy to be stuck in what we learned and identify with our situations, addictions, or labels. As we never know when change will happen, or when we will need to be present, we better get practicing. As the saying goes, "*Champions are made in practice.*" Robin Sharma[24] expresses the practice beautifully: "Champions are made in The Quiet Hours. During the practice times. While they are silently preparing." Wars being fought, people being displaced, natural disasters depriving us of a sense of normalcy, jobs being lost, relationships ending, loved ones dying: Life! We might think that these things will never happen to us, but losing a job can feel as if we are being removed from everything we know and value. Similarly, the death of a loved one can tear us apart. This practice is the action of being in our *inner knowing*, particularly when we cannot bear what is going on. Change, loss, and death are also life. We can face the rough stuff in life from this place of acknowledgement. We can know that the pain is real, and we have other possibilities. I have worked with violence against women issues and seen many mothers being placed in shelters. I have worked with refugees in communities in economic crisis. I am well aware that life is not just turning to myself.

From my own hardships, volunteer work, and professional experience, I have learned that regardless of what is happening, *here* is my moment of power. *Here* I am a victim and a survivor. Both are true. I can create my reality exactly by the way I choose to experience it. The raped women who told their stories at "Take Back the Night" events shared the most horrible abuse that had happened to them to raise awareness to help others. I felt inspired by these women who taught me so much. I have learned that bad shit happens. It is not about *what* happens, but *what I do with it* that changes my own reality.

Fawzia, a refugee mother, described how she ran away from Somalia with three daughters. She walked for two weeks to get to a refugee camp in Kenya. She witnessed her daughters being repeatedly raped along the way. What could possibly have kept Fawzia whole and functional and able to rebuild her life in a foreign country? She taught me more about the importance of *being present* practices than any training ever could. Fawzia created her reality with her every breath. She kept focusing on what was important: being alive. She told her daughters that what these men had done had nothing to do with them. She explained men rape because patriarchic societies let men get away with treating women as objects. They use and abuse them for their fun and pleasure. She told the three girls, the youngest of whom was only ten years old, that only men who are weak abuse, rape, and disrespect women. Fawzia also told her daughters that was why they had to endure the way—so they could have a better life and meet decent men who will love and respect them and treat them as they deserve. If this is not presence— not letting circumstances define them, courage to see them for what they are, the focus to keep going, and choosing what is possible in the moment—then I do not know what is. The word *Fawzia* means *victorious*. For me, she had the presence, the inner knowing that life is not always easy, but she knew it depended on how she danced with it all. Particularly the agony and the torment.

When I say we already have everything in us, it is not because I read this in a book. I practice it. I am not always as victorious or as strong or determined as Fawzia, but I have seen many people being able to survive and thrive even when every odd was against them. By taking it one step at a time, we can heal. Is it always possible? NO! Which is why we must continually come back to *this* moment. This moment is all we have. This is the dance. We practice the moves according to our ability. It is not difficult to learn the steps and moves. As in life, it is mostly a simple 1-2-3 with some twists and turns. Having a baseline can be helpful, but it is not indispensable. Dancing life is the art of integrating what is *here*, who we are now, with what we know. Learning to dance is an individual process as it depends on so many factors. As mentioned previously, life's dance does not require legs or arms. Young babies teach us this. The dance depends on us, our relationship with music, and our willingness to be.

Learning to dance goes beyond moving. This is a crucial skill to learn. Our life is not what we have nor what we do, it is a universe of things happening *here*. We can learn a move and the basic steps, but the way we put it together reflects our unique internal expression. The practice is about what happens before we actually move; it includes the body's ability in this moment. The practice is paying attention to the way this music is felt, including our emotional reaction and our thoughts. These various and unconscious reactions happen before we even move. Practice being aware of this and come back to notice it again and again. This is the practice, for this is the whole dance. The dance itself makes it easier to learn other styles and moves. It is said that practice makes perfect, but I say practice makes it possible and easier to change when life changes. The more I try to fit my learned moves into the music playing, the less the dance flows. I cannot practice choreography for life, but I do encourage everyone to practice these eight steps. Be creative as you create your own unique dance.

1. Acceptance: the recognition of the music playing
2. Turn to yourself
3. Move in three languages: body, emotions, and mind
4. Zoom in and zoom out: come closer and step back
5. Let it flow: remember and reconnect
6. Surrender: you are supported
7. Come back here, again and again
8. Rewrite your own dance with your *Selfprint*

1—Acceptance: The Recognition of the Music Playing

"How can I accept?" is the first question I hear when I explain that acceptance is the basis of my work, the floor that holds everything on it. Acceptance is not something I can actually do, yet it is always there. At first, acceptance is not that simple. It can be challenging depending on what the word *acceptance* means to each one of us and how we relate to that meaning. Most Western patriarchal societies follow the "achieve and conquer" type of mentality. In this context, acceptance becomes unacceptable. It is a sign of a weak character. Acceptance is seen as passive, on the verge of being spineless. On the other hand, we have the demands of the "doing" acceptance as a religious/spiritual obligation, as a superior force making us swallow the despicable. The "turn the other cheek" or the "forgive and forget" to overcome the uncomfortable is something that can create resistance or resentment. Overall, acceptance is not welcomed easily. Now, add these concepts to self-acceptance. It is tough, right? What is acceptance? After fighting the concept for so long, acceptance became for me the eyes that see, the recognition of what is *here*. It is the truth in all its forms which also includes non-acceptance. This is why I use acceptance as the basis of my work. It all starts with you, for without you there is no dance. Can you accept that?

If you know me, you have heard this story. I started fighting acceptance, like so many with whom I share this practice. Jules Wyman was my beautiful and bold mentor and coach who had a new office in York, UK. She challenged me to turn toward acceptance. As I left her office, she told me to start with self-acceptance. I remember wanting to argue back, but my time was up. On my train ride home, I could not stop wondering: How could I accept myself with all my flaws, with all my inabilities and limitations? I cannot accept that. This is why I pay her to help me overcome all these failings. Then I questioned the opposite. If I do accept, what will happen? I will be a good-for-nothing. I will become all my voices, fears, and images threatening me with horrible futures ahead. After all the money, time, and energy I spent to overcome my shortcomings, transform my flaws, and fix my weaknesses, I cannot give up now. I resisted. Acceptance felt like a waste of energy. My mind needed evidence to argue back, so I dove into research, ordered a bunch of books, and started dissecting the topic.

Luckily, I discovered the book *The Deepest Acceptance: Radical Awakening in Ordinary Life* by Jeff Foster. I had only read a few pages when I Googled the author's name. I was profoundly touched by what I had read in his book. Foster was facilitating a seven-day retreat with the same title of the book in South England a couple of weeks later, and I registered. Today, I am so grateful I paid attention to this curiosity and took a step that changed my life forever.

Eleven years later, acceptance is the basis for my daily practice. Simply put, acceptance is recognition of what is happening. Now, I accept (even the parts I struggle to accept), including my upbringing and my religious influences that told me I was born out of sin. I accept social expectations that told me I had to be someone else or be like someone else. School told me I had to know more and that who I was was not good enough. Spirituality told me I had to transcend my body, my humanity. My family told me I had to behave better. Today, I practice this recognition—acceptance of my thoughts, emotions, and memories—of how I lived it all. My self-acceptance practices[25] allow me, little by little, to break free. I cannot break free from my flaws and shortcomings, but I am free to see who I am.[26] What I do with the information is part of the reality I create, but acceptance frees the energy that was trapped resisting what I could not change. This is the self-acceptance floor that catches me even when I trip on my own feet and fall flat on my face.

Acceptance itself changes nothing; what changes is the way we see facts. This recognition of facts is an open door to possibilities. In acceptance, we welcome everything, not because it is pleasant or unpleasant, but because it is *here*. An earthquake is not pleasant. I have no power to reject it, but I can recognize it for what it is. Identifying the event as an earthquake helps me know what my responsibility is in responding. I can then ask myself, what is the smallest step I can take, *here*, to dance with it as-is? This is why acceptance is the floor for our dance. With a floor underneath us, it is easier to accept an invitation to dance. Once I recognize it as active information, I can use this information to my benefit. Acceptance says this is the music that is playing. This is me *here*. I have choices about it and how I want to dance it. I can even decide whether to dance at all. This too is accepting life's invitation, to be part of it, to turn toward it and live fully.

2—Turn to Yourself

The first invitation to practice is to recognize and accept what is. The second invitation is to turn to yourself.

As I arrive at the clinic's gate in Cascais, Portugal, I see Sara, my next client, parking her car. I stop and wave as I wait for her to cross the street. As Sara waves in response, she laughs and turns her palm toward her face saying, "It is not like this, but like this." Having been working online for over twelve years now, I have learned to use non-verbal cues to emphasize what seems relevant. Turning my palm to my face reminds me to check in,[27] and I ask clients to play with it too. Sara continues to let me know, as she crosses the street, that she remembered to turn to herself a few days back when, while rushing through her chores, her daughter needed attention. Sara's reaction to her daughter was to tell her how much she already has, but she remembered, stopped, and turned to herself to check in. She tells me, "I just saw your palm turning." Sara continues, "I noticed how guilty I feel for working too much. I saw memories of my relationship with my mother and how I realized I compensate by giving my daughter everything material. I felt so bad that I stopped what I was doing and we played together." I thank Sara for sharing her experience and for having the courage to turn to herself and accept what she saw as information.

Turning inward can put us in contact with some discomfort, but fear not. We can learn to hold discomfort in a healthy way. Some people are unaware of old wounds or even traumas that were unconsciously repressed. By slowing down and noticing what is *here*, we can reconnect with old traumas. If this is the case, please, ask for professional help. Trauma is serious and there are many effective ways to work with the multiple forms trauma can take. Peter Levine,[28] a trauma therapist and the creator of Somatic Experiencing, borrowed the term *titration* from chemistry to define the pace needed to deal with trauma. Titration is a series of micro additions with intervals for observation. It is a small, slow-paced contact with what is there, respecting individual time, and allowing interruptions for micro adjustments. When we turn inward, we never know what we are about to find, and so, the best approach is to do so in very small steps. We can be brave and curious to see what is *here*, but we must be kind and patient in case we need to stop or even step back from what we find. This gradual and gentle dance teaches us to respect the music we hear. Shedding light into our inner worlds opens doors to major parts that are alive inside and are calling for our attention. Most of us do not even notice that so much is happening in our bodies. When we are not in our bodies, our minds take over and dictate the learned moves—the perceived "shoulds." The mind cannot feel the music. It evaluates, analyzes, and judges everything from the song to the way we dance. The mind will bring up images of past experiences just to convince us to keep doing what we have learned. The mind has a role, which it does well, and that role is to keep us busy, distracted, and not in our bodies. Can you come back to the body?

Curiosity is the best ingredient of this practice. I try to be curious, caring, and creative as I observe myself and ask, what is *here*? This question alone changes my focus from the distractions to my embodied presence. The question expands our vision to see beyond the obvious, notice the old patterns, and dive into inner self-discovery. Turning to myself is the ultimate expedition. What will I find in this inner adventure? What do I need? Willingness to *dance*. I will find the rest as I explore. So far, I have found creativity, resilience, resourcefulness, true confidence, respect for self, and differentiation. I have also found trauma, covered in fight, flight, or freeze responses. I found sadness and my long-lost friend, anger, and so much more. Inner adventures are not always easy. Are you up for it?

I remember a particular session I had with Matt Licata, my therapist at the time, during which I said I did not want to do this work anymore. He listened with a smile, opening space for my own decision. At this moment, I remembered that no matter how difficult that moment was, it was not as hard as all the fighting, the running away, the struggles of trying to cope. So, I kept showing up for practice. *Being aware* as a practice puts me in the driver's seat, because I can catch myself, my emotions, and my thoughts before they speak on my behalf. Turning inward shows me my own predetermined programs, my ignorance, and the ways in which I am not prepared to be *here* now. I have spent most of my life doing the exact opposite. I have focused exclusively on something outside of myself.

Sara experienced this as she practiced turning inward. She did not see anything she did not already know, but noticing, in the moment, shifted her focus to the reality she wanted to create as opposed to continuing to live in automatic mode. That is why this is a practice. Sara needs to keep turning to herself and notice what thoughts and meanings surface, in each moment. Sara shared that at work she was seeing how she avoids conflict. Turning inward is helping her hear the voices inside saying she will not be liked, trusted, or valued. Sara is catching her fear of people finding out that maybe she is not as competent as they think, her images of rejection as others realize she is not like them, and the isolation that she will never belong. Sara once noticed how she avoids making decisions and how her body temperature would rise when faced with decision making. On that day, Sara shared that she received an email and felt afraid. She stopped and checked the reply in her head, trying to avoid any possible conflict. As Sara felt this happening in her head, her heartbeat began accelerating and her muscles tensed up. Sara was not sure whether she was feeling this fast beat because she was afraid or because she was excited that she had noticed. She smiled and wrote a very different email. Her new email took her a long time to finish, but she included her opinion and her truth. Sara is noticing her learned strategies to avoid conflict: how she avoided situations, lied because of it, blamed herself, and then compensated. Sara says that turning in toward herself is letting her clean the house—her inner house. That is our work together.

This practice helps us see ourselves think, feel, and sense. We get to know ourselves from the inside out. Sometimes, turning inward can feel like learning a foreign language. It is easier when we are in the country immersed in it, making mistakes, but practicing every day.

3—Dance in Three Languages: Body, Emotions, and Mind

Getting lost in translation is easy. I am not fluent in these three languages, and when I am competent, I often let the mind speak for the heart or body sensations. I grew up surrounded by finger pointing images of the superiority of the left brain hemisphere. The oppressive control of one aspect of the mind narrows my living experience. After years of practice, I still have to be mindful of this internalized ideal demanding me to ignore heart and body. That is why *Here*, I am inviting you to learn these three languages and become so fluent that you feel like a native.

The Language of the Mind

Faith is venting her work frustrations about a dysfunctional company and an incompetent boss. When I ask her where she feels this in her body, she immediately makes a disappointed face. She shakes her head and tells me, "I never know what to answer when you ask 'where in the body stuff.'" I understand and say it is okay not to know. My question is just an invitation for her to turn her attention to the body. She does not need to know how to put it into words. Faith struggles a bit as she answers and says, "I don't know, here maybe." She points to her heart area.

The mind is amazing. That is why it is fun to learn about how the mind works including what it does and why. Once we know how something functions, we can use it better, just like a machine. The mind is constantly analyzing, judging, bringing images that relate, and comparing and contrasting as it decides. Knowing this about the mind helps us ask better questions. Do you know someone who has a super smart phone and only uses it to text or make calls? Do you think it is a waste to have a smart phone and not use its full capabilities? Let us not do the same with our minds. Nowadays, cognitive dissonance, first named by the social psychologist Leon Festinger, seems to be a widespread problem. This psychological stress happens when there is discrepancy between what people believe and how they choose to behave. It creates the tension we feel when we cannot align a positive image of ourselves with our behavior. Learning to notice our own incongruity can reduce tension and diminish our need to look for confirmation bias. Regardless, whether these processes happen unconsciously or the objective of the mind is to control the tension felt, what matters is that our mind increases our capacity to hold tension as we recognize that opposite ideas can carry truth.

Are you willing to learn the mind's language? For example, asking good questions expands our ability to think critically, to be mentally active, and catch our own young tendencies. Asking *"why"* questions shrinks prospects. All questions can be useful at some point, but start with what you really want. Ask *"what"* only after you ask *"how."* Save the *"why"* for big *whys*, such as *Why am I here?* The mind wants to solve and that turns everything into an action, which then becomes a never-ending, exhausting circle.

When I ask *Why is this happening to me?* my mind will get into an incessant quest to find reasons and excuses: "It's because I am a woman, I'm old, I'm a foreigner, I'm this or that..." Asking *why* will not expand my possibilities, but it will keep me spinning in place. Instead, if I ask *What is happening?* my mind will start listing, identifying, naming, and noticing everything that is happening. *"What"* questions will bring me back to the present moment, to more tangible facts, and I will have much more information to play with and, from there, concrete possibilities for action. With these doable answers, I can follow up and ask *how*, but only once I can start with one of the *whats*. How can this information be useful for me and others? This question narrows my focus, making room for me to see my emotions. Are the questions you are asking bringing you back to the moment of clear possibilities?

The Language of Emotions

Faith's mind is trying to solve a problem that she cannot solve, which is her company and her boss's competence. Faith is tired. Her mind is going around in circles, analyzing, and looking for reasons. She remembers many years back when she first joined the company, how her previous boss who recruited her admired her work, trusted her, and supported her initiatives. However, that boss is no longer with the company. Her mind is exhausted. Emotionally, Faith is feeling more than she can hold: frustration, anger, and sadness for the lost work environment. There is also fear about the future and disgust for incompetence. All these emotions are asking for attention, but Faith's mind is trying to make them go away by trying to solve what she cannot control. As a result, Faith gets trapped in this loop and feels exhausted.

Have you ever tried to control your emotions? Our emotions have a life of their own. When left unsupervised, they can destroy our day. Like children, our emotions want attention, care, and support. Learning the language of emotions takes practice. Understanding what an emotion is asking for is important, so we are not misled by the images the mind creates. I asked Faith, "What do your emotions want or need right now? What is the underlying request for you to feel?" Faith said her frustration and anger wanted her to give up because it was too much. I asked her for an emotion. Faith stopped and said that her anger wanted her to feel calm and protected. It was a request for her to enjoy herself and feel relaxed. Once Faith realized that her emotions supported her own good, she felt empowered to create a strategy to bring more joy into her workday.

Do you have emotions that are dominating your life? Emotions can keep us hostage, draining us of useful energy and the ability to respond to situations. Hence the invitation for us to learn to look at emotions, notice their shape, intensity, and movement, and get into a relationship with them. We can gain an ability to listen to what these emotions are trying to ask of us. In the book *The Language of Emotions: What Your Feelings are Trying to Tell You*, Karla McLaren, M.Ed., social science researcher, and award-winning author, denounces our tendency to value pleasant emotions more than unpleasant emotions and distance ourselves from that fact that all emotions are important messengers of equal importance. When we listen to all emotions, each one becomes a source of energy and a doorway to self-discovery and inner wisdom. If you experience intense emotions, particularly when allowing yourself to feel repressed or disowned emotions, reach out and ask for professional help. I too ask for help, all the time. Sometimes, we just need someone to be there and witness the process with us, someone who can hold space for us and feel what we cannot face alone. Being *here*—emotions and all— brings us to our bodies: a place as vast as the universe itself.

The Language of the Body

Are you aware of your own body language? Body language is overly used in sales, business, and the corporate world, mainly to control first impressions during interview processes or sales pitches. Paying attention to our nonverbal communication is important, but for the practice we are developing *here*, it is necessary to get in touch with our own inner sensations of our body. Learning to control body language without being consciously aware of our body sensations is like trying to dance without having ever heard music. Our physical bodies use our five senses—sight, sound, smell, touch, and taste—to gather information and communicate through sensations. Body sensations are a fluid, complex language that is constantly communicating with us. We can venture into this universe; however, most of us have never traveled that far. We work our bodies at the gym, we wrap our bodies with clothes, yet most of us are illiterate when it comes to listening to our bodies and sensing this language. By default, humans are designed to look for pleasure and run away from pain. This is an automatic program. Nevertheless, people often are much more fluent in painful and unpleasant sensations than pleasant ones. The practice is not to control or make our bodies do anything, but to pay attention to the ever-so-slight sensations already happening. What sensations can you notice?

We can practice feeling sensations with a quick body scan. Start by feeling your feet on the ground and notice the sensations. Move up your feet, toward your legs, upper body, etc. Sense each part of your body. Notice the temperature on your skin. Notice differences in temperature in different parts of your body. Notice the qualities, the texture. Is it tingling, pulsating, tight, sore? Does it have movement? If so, in what direction? Is it contracting, dense, throbbing, or expanding? Is it wobbly, burning, itchy, heavy, or light? Is it dull? Sense: do not try to change it or control it. Just play with noticing. Come back to it and start again. Practice watching from inside out, slowly but steadily. It takes time to learn a new language, keep practicing. Pick just one practice and be consistent. Sometimes, we need to come closer to get to know all the details, but other times it is too much and we step back to gain a little perspective. Once we get familiar with the sensations, then we might want to attempt to gain some vocabulary and put these sensations into words and feel them. As we begin to become fluent in each language, listening to what is underneath, to truly connect empathically with ourselves, in a non-violent[29] way, then we will see these three languages are actually saying the same. This distinction is only to facilitate our understanding.

4—Zoom In and Zoom Out: Come Closer and Step Back

Zoom in and zoom out has been my go-to, quick and simple way to regain ground when I am overwhelmed by what is happening. I cannot dance unless I understand and feel the music playing.

Five years ago, I started a long weekend workshop in Lisbon, Portugal, by asking people to state a problem. I projected a closeup photo of a huge fresh cow dung. My intention was not to gross people out, but to make this practice clear. I asked participants to see that image as their problem. I asked them to view their problem as that huge cow dung, whether it was an incompetent boss or a relationship issue. Now, I told them, imagine you are forced to come closer, closer, even closer, so close that your vision field only sees cow dung, nothing else. Zoom in really close. It stinks. And if you get too close, it will stick to your clothes and skin. You get the picture, right? This is what we do when we only think about our problem. We talk about it constantly and amplify it so much that it becomes larger than us. We zoom in so much, and so fast, that we lose perspective on what else is there.

On the next slide, I had a photo of the same cow dung, but this time I zoomed out. The photo showed a beautiful green field covered with flowers, cows, and the ocean view at a distance. We could still see the same cow dung, but its weight on the scenery was completely appropriate. When I zoomed out, I could see the reason the fields were so rich and lush. The proposed exercise was for participants to see their chosen problem in several stages of zooming in and zooming out. After we finished the exercise, people shared what had changed for them as they zoomed in and zoomed out on their problems. Both perspectives are real and true, and both are needed. In the first photo, we could even see green flies and tiny larvae. This level of detail can be quite useful and that is why we sometimes need to get close. However, we cannot stay there too long. We need to zoom out too and take both perspectives into account.

I do not create recipes for my clients to follow. Each life is so dynamic and alive that the recipe that I need right now might not be useful later on. Nevertheless, I will share an example of how I dance and evaluate when my face is in cow dung. My red flags show me I need to zoom out when:

1. My thought patterns are too intense
2. I want to fix "a problem" that does not depend on me
3. I catch myself talking about it all the time
4. My attitude is too rigid; I am unwilling to even listen to others' opinions
5. I need or feel absolute certainty
6. I feel so uncomfortable in a situation that I lose perspective of the other as a human being just like myself
7. My beliefs seem to be either/or with no space in between for uncertainty
8. My emotions are on an utmost high

Ten years ago, when I first used the zoom in and zoom out with the cow dung image, what I did not know was that this strategy had the same effect as pendulation. Levine[30] uses *pendulation* as a way to invite clients to shift their awareness from what is becoming unbearable for the system, to paying attention to something else that is easier for the system to hold, something pleasant. This backward-and-forward swing has tremendous benefits for healing. By zooming in and out, we gain awareness of what else is available. It turns the unconscious conscious. Pendulation allows our body to simultaneously integrate the multitude of things that we are already capable of experiencing. Shifting our attention enables us to connect with ourselves as well as with what is around us. The main goal of pendulation is to teach a trauma client to learn to self-regulate and feel more empowered dealing with symptoms. Overall, when we *dance* this in and out, we can notice the resources already available inside as well as outside. Just like a dance.

When we dance, we do not just walk or run in one direction. We move forward and backward. We turn and keep moving. In life, staying too zoomed in while dealing with a problem serves no one. The mind wants to solve it fast, so it insists we keep thinking about it; but, it is much more beneficial to step back, zoom out, and see the same situation from a different angle. With new information, we broaden our thinking, open up possibilities, and allow our dance to flow.

5—Let it Flow: Remember and Reconnect

We cannot prevent the unpredictable flow that is life. Yet, we resist it. It is a natural reaction to protect us from the unfamiliar.

Lynn's boss just told her she cannot guarantee her position—another layer of the pandemic and insecurities of 2020. Halfway through her list of uncertainties, Lynn remembers her previous job transition. She smiles tenderly saying, "If anyone had told me ten years ago that losing my job would have led me to the life of service I live now, I would have said they were crazy. Back then, I thought I was too old to learn new skills. I didn't believe it could happen, but it did. I changed completely, and I lived these last ten years so intensely on so many levels. I found purpose, and I found myself." Just this memory brings Lynn back to her own knowing. Her facial expression opens up and her eyes smile as she lists all the things she could not believe were possible and yet had happened. The memory reconnected Lynn with a sense of possibilities *here* too.

There is so much happening at each moment, outside as well as inside our bodies. *This* moment contains past, future, present, and everything else right now. Lynn was just going through the motions of her situation. When change happens, like the 2020 pandemic, there is a great deal of uncertainty. When we go through pain, old wounds reopen. We scream, we run away, and we want to fight. Our desire to get rid of the discomfort is natural, as is the shame we feel, the guilt, and even our sadness. One challenging situation can bring to the surface former similar events. It is a natural flow of our mortal selves, this cycle from birth to death. This is why, I believe that **owning our mortality and *seeing it for what it is, rather than fearing it,* saves us every time.** Our mortality reminds us to be in love with life itself. As Lynn described her discomfort in that moment, her past pains and discomforts came to memory. When she allowed the memories to flow, she grew open to possibilities in the moment. As she remembered, Lynn touched a fear from her past, but her body also saw that success was a part of the flow. This is the richness of embracing apparent opposites and allowing them to flow.

It is the awareness, in this moment, that reconnects us with our natural essence in regard to events and emotions. This awareness does not create flow. Awareness is what notices the flow reconnecting us with our bodies and its alive wisdom. From *here* we can take in the lessons, facts, and experiences. Lynn just showed us this practice. She recognized what was happening, insecurities and all, and as she turned to herself, she moved to the music of her three languages. Lynn could zoom in and feel the fear of the imaginary future, but the natural flow took her to the inevitable zoom out and broadened the perspectives that she also gained from her past experience. The practice allowed her to reconnect and remember herself for who she was: her *Selfprint*, her inner power.

The dance requires remembering all the parts. As Levine explains, to remember is a *Somatic Experiencing* happening in the body. It occurs when we embody all that is ours. Egyptian Goddess Isis became known for giving soul, to resurrect, her dismembered husband by putting all his pieces back together again. Life, to let the dance flow, is to collect all the scattered pieces of our stories, including the lost memories, desires, and traumas in the body. We must collect the old beliefs and values, the dreams and illusions, and see them all here as well. We must show up and leave nothing behind, just as Lynn did. When Lynn was present with all her stories, she noticed how much room she had for it all. That is why her posture shifted and her smile widened. It was as if she had found more space inside herself to access all other parts that were already there. It was there all along, within her, and I was a witness holding space with her.

Lynn flowed between past and present emotions and remembered the past possibilities that brought her to that moment. Her mind screamed, "Are you insane? You have so much to do. You have to find a solution, to fix it, to control it!" In her body now she knows this dance, this music, this moment, and Lynn's dance continues. She can perceive all as music and has learned to dance accordingly.

6—Surrender: You Are Supported

Nature does nothing and
yet leaves nothing undone.

—Lao Tzu

This practice is the easiest one and the hardest for our nervous system to understand. We learn that we need to do and accomplish, but then need to surrender. Can both be true? Can we act, create, and contribute while we live as nature? Can we allow the cycles of life's dance? I believe we can, but it is an acquired skill and takes practice. The human nervous system is wired for connection, which is how we learn to regulate our emotional state. We need contact and need to be seen, to develop the ability to self-regulate. As babies, we sense others' emotions, which becomes what we know. We need others to help us make sense of what these emotions are and what they mean. Unfortunately, most of us are ill-equipped to self-regulate. This is by no intended fault of our caretakers, as they likely had less than we did.

As babies and children, we need to learn nearly everything. Physically, our primary caretakers feed and shelter us, while teaching us to feed and clothe ourselves. Emotionally, we also need to be shown how to identify and understand how to experience our emotions in a way that is healthy for us. Babies copy and reflect, which is why we need someone to mirror us back. This support is essential for a healthy nervous system. We need to be seen, held, and loved. These are basic human needs, and we will find a way to get these needs met, either from our caretakers or our immediate surroundings. Sometimes, we look outside ourselves and meet our needs with possessions or substances. One way or another, most of our behaviors are requests of an emotional need.

When we are not aware of our own needs, we do not notice that what we are doing serves that purpose. Whether we are workaholics, perfectionists, or laissez-faire, we unconsciously try to manage our nervous system, to feel supported. We are constantly trying to self-regulate our inner world. Self-regulation is our ability to monitor, assess, and modify our emotional response to experiences. Regardless of what strategies we learn from an early age, we use a combination of strategies as we grow and develop. For example, distraction is known to alleviate emotional distress and even reduce the intensity of pain. Worrying and rumination are both attempts to problem solve and are often considered a maladaptive emotion regulation. Positive, good-spirited humor can be an effective strategy, but when we use negative and mean humor, this coping tool is less effective. Distancing can reduce reactivity from negative stimuli and therefore regulate the emotional response. Other strategies that interfere with our ability to self-regulate are sleep (particularly REM sleep), food, exercise, and the use of substances. Understanding our needs and how we experience our body sensations can help us find healthier ways to meet these needs and self-regulate. However, trying to control our needs creates less room to experience our natural system, and then we get into a downward spiral where we fight to control the uncontrollable. The more we fight our system, the less we feel supported. As in nature, the answer is not to control. The answer is to notice our own unconsciously learned strategies. By understanding the intention of each strategy, we are listening to the music. We are accepting what is being asked. Relinquishing control requires not doing whatever we have learned. Rather, it is being with the request and dancing with it in a way that is supportive of our nervous systems. How do you support your nervous system?

Mindful-based practices have this invitation to surrender. When I first read *The Surrender Experiment* by Martin Singer, I was not convinced. Being a true story, it made me curious enough to play with it. The more I surrender, the more I can see and feel how supported I am. It is a slow and irregular process, a dance between the habit of control and the tiny attempts to notice first, to touch it, and to let go. It takes practice to trust this moment and not jump back into the mind's attempts to keep us safe from emotional discomfort. It is exhausting to want control. It is also unfulfilling and never enough. The more I noticed how I want to control everything, the more I identified these strategies with clients. Farrah is an example of someone who learned to distract herself with work, control every detail of her life, and always be positive.

Farrah was the personification of her name; she was joy in human form. But Farrah was losing her spark because she was overworked and exhausted. Her body was collapsing on her and her mind could not see a way out. She needed to work and she loved the intensity of the travel and the frenetic nature of being responsible for a large number of international groups. Farrah came to see me at the recommendation of a good friend. She was apprehensive with this coaching practice since her friend told her that she did not need to do more work.

In our sessions, Farrah gave herself permission to play with the process I offered her. During her deathbed exercise, she saw herself having time for herself and time to do the things she loves. Farrah surrendered to what she felt and remembered having once left a job that led her to her current successful career. Remembering her past connected her with this inner knowing that she has been supported and guided, even against all odds. The more she connected with this sense of being supported, the luckier she felt. Her word was luck. Farrah started by listing people and events that were supportive of her. She surrendered to the idea of how the support looked and got in touch with this sense of support. The more she felt it, the more convinced she was that she had to turn in her letter of resignation. She surrendered to her truth and acted on it. We created a goal to find the appropriate time for her to finish her commitments to train someone for her position and to communicate about her leaving the team that had supported her.

Sometimes practice is totally somatic; other times, it happens as we discuss issues. Sometimes, we feel it and other times we lose it, which is why it is a practice. As a workaholic and a perfectionist of every detail, Farrah was trying to self-regulate her nervous system. We cannot go from one extreme to the other. Surrender practice is not always a fixed linear action. To surrender is to know your history while letting go of it at the same time. It is owning your before and after, while living this tiny sensation that life itself has been *here* for you, with you, and as you. Farrah could not have predicted what happened next, but when the next phase came, she was present and observing. She took one step in the direction her old lady in her deathbed had shown her. This is what I practice and share. The dance brings you back, again and again, to this moment of power already *here*.

7—Come Back Here, Again and Again

How do you feel about repetition? Repetition is the heart of dancing and of this practice. Move forward and backward, go somewhere else, and come back *here*. There are endless techniques to choose from when getting started. My favorite practice is easy and always available. It is focusing on my inhale and exhale. No matter where I am, no matter what I am doing, I can always turn my focus to my breathing. I can notice the air going into my nostrils, and the air traveling into my body. I can notice the temperatures in different places and notice what expands and what contracts. I do not have to do anything because it all happens inside of my body. This breathing is just life, and the more detailed I can be in my observations, the easier it is to be present. And yet, it takes practice. My breathing is a mindfulness practice.

If focusing on the breath is too much, please respect this resistance, but do not let that stop you. There are so many practices to help us come back *here*, again and again, with soft attention. The trick is to find the one that is most supportive for where we are in our current lives. Walking, mindful movement, and dance can be great ways for those of us who cannot stand still. Just like with dancing, we all have our favorite moves. That is the best place to start. Being inspired by what speaks to us, and making it ours with small steps, works wonders. My first real practice was with the traffic light meditation. It is a method that only takes the brief moments we spend when we are stopped at a red light. With our eyes open, we look at the red light while focusing on our breathing. That is it. It is easy and safe. Because we are stopped for the red light, we know it will be short, so there is less danger. Our mind does not create a thousand lists of things we should be doing right now. This is a short practice, but let us not underestimate the value of these short experiences in our body, especially if repeated, when we have to drive through many traffic lights. If we do not drive or do not have traffic lights during our commutes, we can choose something that we do multiple times a day that could offer a few minutes of mindfulness. Will you give it a try?

Washing hands, for example. Washing our hands, or a similar action, does not require much of our attention. We can set an intention to practice when we take an elevator or wait for appointments. Children can be great reminders and teachers of coming back to this moment. Presence is our natural state, although I did not believe it when I first heard it since this step was so difficult for me. Nevertheless, presence has all the qualities that children naturally do. Presence is having a beginner's mind, unknowing, a state of curiosity about this moment. Presence is embodiment, and children are highly connected with their bodies. They jump, skip, and move freely, as if doing what the body feels like doing. They are not in their heads. When they play, they do not play to have something done, to accomplish, or achieve. They are in the moment, enjoying themselves, and having fun. Also, children seem to have this sense of wonder, this ability to be anything their hearts call for in that moment. They pretend to be animals or robots alike, no judgement of what is possible or not. From *here* we can notice the multitude of our beings and see how whole we are. Coming back to this moment allows us to see the meaning we give to things and explore how we are creating our reality. The practice offers so many benefits, but we must choose to return to this little moment. For this is the ever-first step where we can continue to rewrite our story.

8—Rewrite Your Own Dance with Your *Selfprint*

Ready to rewrite your dance? I rewrite mine with every breath, although sometimes less consciously than I would like.

I have been noticing how I smile at the fact that I am writing a book. If this is not rewriting my own story in and of itself, I do not know what is. I learned that I cannot write. I learned this when I was six years old with Irma Maria de Deus, Sister Mary of God, whom I called Mary of the devil, but that is another story. The stories we experience live in our body's memory. The mind interprets the best it can and assigns meanings, which either open or close opportunities for us. When I look back, I can see these filters and the shame that made it impossible for me to be present with my experience. Nevertheless, I cannot change my past. I can only be *here* with my choices, now, one step at a time. Breaking it down to what is possible gives me room to notice the differences between my body sensations, my mind, a feeling, or an emotion. When it is too much to hold, and I feel too many emotions at once, I remind myself to slow down, be kind, take some time, breathe, go for a walk, or ask for help.

My practice is to notice old thoughts and beliefs that affirm *I cannot write*. I can sense the emotions that arise. These three languages are life savers for my neglected nervous system. *Here*, I can zoom in and feel the weight of the belief that I do not have what it takes, that this is an insurmountable task, that it is not possible. When I zoom out, I see possibilities. I see that I have achieved many apparently impossible undertakings before. I also see what I have learned: the secret has always been returning to this moment, where I have a choice. This being *here* shows me the flow of my number eight, including my past and future, my illusions, and false dreams of who I should be. That is when I remember my uniqueness. That is when I reconnect with what is mine already and when I reconnect with my clients who ask me to have something for them to remind themselves.

When I reconnect with them, I remember all the books I have read, and I know each one has touched something within me, something that was mine and wanted to be heard. This is what I hope to achieve by writing this book.

As I surrender, I notice I have room to give myself permission to not have to write this book. In writing this book, I kept coming back to the keyboard, asking for help, and accepting support from those who know what they are doing. I have learned to trust the process, one word at a time. I rewrite as often as I need to. I have the ability to write this book. This life of mine has many ups and downs, realizations, missteps, mistakes, and times of awareness. My life is my own discombobulated dance, and this is how I rewrite my own story over and over again. This is my practice and my suggestion for you. Getting there by being *here*, even if it is only for a split second.

⊛

Homeplay

If the above practice tips are not enough and you want to add possibilities, play with the following questions:

1. What does the word *"acceptance"* mean to you? Jot down a few examples.
2. As you turn to yourself, what is present and alive for you now?
3. Can you point out one sensation in your body, one thought or belief, and one emotion?

8

Conclusion

Freedom is not given to us by anyone;
we have to cultivate it ourselves.
It is a daily practice...
No one can prevent you from being aware of
each step you take or each breath in and
breath out.

—THICH NHAT HANH

The Dance Without a Name

Once, a client told me that when she started this practice she felt like a dismantled skeleton of a former self and that I had taught her how to sing the song to restore her bones.[31] I love this image. What more can we want but to know how to collect our disintegrated parts and remember that this too is life? Life can become demanding. I get it. It is because I know this, and live it, that I have shared my struggles as well as

153

my most reliable practices. When I turned my focus away from outcomes alone and brought my attention back to being present, I saw new potential. The practices that have helped me most are the ones that respect my own nature to flow and dance. We all have a choice: we can continue to do what we have always done and complain about what is, fight it or avoid it all together, or choose something else. There comes a time when we know we must stop repeating the same things and expecting different results. That is the time to notice. We must be willing to change if we want to live in respect of our true nature and feel connected with ourselves and our lives, even in the discomfort.

This practice assigns no blame or shame, although these arise as a part of the dance. In facing them, we use curiosity, respect, and kindness. We also need courage. It takes work to recognize the programs running in our background. Getting to know ourselves, without believing every thought we have, requires commitment and a willingness to flow in the apparent paradoxes that we experience. If I could ask you to take one thing from this book, it would be the sensations you get when something touches you deeply, those moments when you feel free and alive. For me this happens when I dance and when I watch a sunrise. This is the *Selfprint*: what is touched in this unique way. It is yours. It is the feeling that there is no past, no future. The head wants to call our attention, the body is bursting with sensations, and our emotions respond to both. We see the figure 8 flowing, touching it all. We reconnect to the flow, and we remember that, even though we might not have everything we need in life, we already have what it takes to be *here*. In this moment, we touch ∞, the whole universe. As we allow it, and surrender because there is nothing else to do, the mind may fill up with thoughts.

We thank the mind for the reminders, and we act with what we know is for us, now.

I have used *"we"* throughout the book because this is my practice as well. The *"we"* I use honors how individual you and I are in our unique experience. This practice is knowing that we can see things as both separate and different as well as the same. The dance allows us to see inside ourselves, so we can see outside ourselves. The integration between the figure 8 and the ∞ is the integration we are looking for in ourselves and in the world. People say, "But there are injustices in the world; there are abuses and wars." It is true, but by being *here*, we can choose what we must fight for and how can we fight. Life does not exclude, and dancing life means aligning our actions with our emotions and our thoughts while remembering what this is all about.

Allow me to ask you one last favor: please practice. Practice the song that restores life, your song that flows and touches everything in you. I have been seeing this in myself and in those with whom I work. We really do not want to be perfect. We are longing for our *Selfprint here*. This is what will burst open old beliefs and false ideas that we have to be something else. This practice does not take much time. It is ever so subtle, so small, so simple. Come closer and touch this moment. Zoom out and see yourself in your last minute of life. When you look back onto this life of yours, what is it that you want to feel about your life? Do not let current events, wars, earthquakes, or pandemics determine how you feel about your life. Because what really matters in the end is how you collected your bones, sang your song, and allowed life to dance you.

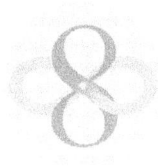

Bibliography

Adyashanti. *Emptiness Dancing.* Boulder, CO: Sounds
True, 2006.

Adyashanti. *The End of Your World: Uncensored Straight
Talk on the Nature of Enlightenment.* Boulder,
CO: Sounds True, 2008.

Adyashanti. *Falling into Grace: Insights on the End
of Suffering.* Boulder, CO: Sounds True, 2011.

Arnold Ventures. "Evidence Based Strategies for Abatement
of Harms from the Opioid Epidemic." Carnevale
Associates LLC. November 10, 2020.

Atewand, Attul. *Being Mortal: Medicine and What Matters
in the End.* New York: Metropolitan Books, 2014.

Auton, Adam et al., "A Global Reference for Human Genetic
Variation." *Nature* 526, no. 7571 (2015): 68–74.

Brach, Tara. *Radical Self-Acceptance: A Buddhist Guide
to Freeing Yourself from Shame.* Audio CD. Boulder,
CO: Sounds True, 2004.

Braden, Gregg. *Fractal Time: The Secret of 2012 and a New World Age.* Carlsbad, CA: Hay House, 2009.

Baer, Drake. "Kahneman: Your Cognitive Biases Act Like Optical Illusions." The Cut. January 13, 2017. https://www.thecut.com/2017/01/kahneman-biases-act-like-optical-illusions.html

Brown, Brené. *I Thought It Was Just Me (but it isn't): Telling the Truth about Perfectionism, Inadequacy, and Power.* New York: Gotham Books, 2007.

Brown, Brené. *The Gifts of Imperfection: Let Go of Who You Think You're Supposed to Be and Embrace Who You Are.* Center City, MN: Hazelden Publishing, 2010.

Brown, Brené. *Daring Greatly: How the Courage to Be Vulnerable Transforms the Way We Live, Love, Parent, and Lead.* New York: Penguin Random House, 2012.

Brown, Brené. *The Power of Vulnerability: Teachings on Authenticity, Connection and Courage.* Audio CD. Boulder, CO: Sounds True, 2012.

Brown, Brené. *Dare to Lead: Brave Work. Tough Conversations. Whole Hearts.* New York: Penguin Random House, 2018.

Brown, Brené. *Braving the Wilderness: The Quest for True Belonging and the Courage to Stand Alone.* New York: Random House, 2019.

Buchard, Brendon. *Life's Golden Ticket: A Story about Second Chances.* San Francisco, CA: HarperOne, 2016.

Buckingham, Marcus. *Go Put Your Strengths to Work; 6 Powerful Steps to Achieve Outstanding Performance.* New York: Free Press, 2010.

Chödrön, Pema. *When Things Fall Apart: Heart Advice for Difficult Times.* London: Harper Collins, 2005.

Chödrön, Pema. *Comfortable with Uncertainty: 108 Teachings on Cultivating Fearlessness and Compassion*. Edited by Emily Hilburn Sell. Boulder, CO: Shambala, 2010.

Chödrön, Pema. *Welcoming the Unwelcome: Wholehearted Living in a Brokenhearted World*. Boulder, CO: Shambala, 2019.

Coelho, Paulo. *The Pilgrimage*. Translated by Alan R. Clarke. New York: HarperOne, 2008.

Damásio, António. *O Livro da Consciência: A Construção do cérebro Consciente*. Lisboa: Círculo de Leitores, 2010.

Damásio, António. O Erro de Descartes. *Emoção, razão e Cérebro Humano*. Lisboa: Publicações Europa-América, 14ᵗʰ Edição, 1995.

De Mello, Anthony. *Awareness: The Perils and Opportunities of Reality*. New York: Image, 1992.

Doidge, Norman. *The Brain That Changes Itself: Stories of Personal Triumph from the Frontiers of Brain Science*. London: Penguin Books, 2007.

Foster, Jeff. *The Wonder of Being: Awakening to an Intimacy Beyond Words*. Salisbury, UK: Non-Duality Press, 2010.

Foster, Jeff. *The Deepest Acceptance: Radical Awakening in Ordinary Life*. Boulder, CO: Sounds True, 2012.

Foster, Jeff. *Falling in Love with Where You Are: A Year of Prose and Poetry on Radically Opening Up to the Pain and Joy of Life*. Salisbury, UK: Non-Duality Press, 2013.

Foster, Jeff. *The Way of Rest: Finding the Courage to Hold Everything in Love*. Boulder, CO: Sounds True, 2016.

Foster, Jeff. *You Were Never Broken: Poems to Save your Life*. Boulder, CO: Sounds True, 2020.

Goleman, Daniel. *Emotional Intelligence: Why It Can Matter More Than IQ*. London: Bloomsbury, 1996.

Grout, Pam. *E-Squared: Nine Do-it-Yourself Energy Experiments that Prove Your Thoughts Create Your Reality*. London: Hay House, 2013.

Holmes, Thomas H., and Richard H. Rahe. "The Social Readjustment Rating Scale." *Journal of Psychosomatic Research*, 11, no. 2 (1967): 213–218.

Kahneman, Daniel. *Thinking, Fast and Slow*. New York: Farrar, Straus and Giroux, 2013.

Levine, Peter A. *Waking the Tiger: Healing Trauma, The Innate Capacity to Transform Overwhelming Experiences*. Berkley, CA: North Atlantic Books, 1997.

Licata, Matt. *The Path is Everywhere: Uncovering the Jewels Hidden Within You*. Boulder, CO: Wandering Yogi Press, 2017.

Lightman, Alan. *Einstein's Dreams*. New York: Warner Books, 1994.

Lipton, Bruce H. *The Biology of Belief: Unleashing the Power of Consciousness, Matter & Miracles*. Carlsbad, CA: Hay House, 2008.

McLaren, Karla. *The Language of Emotions: What Your Feelings are Trying to Tell You*. Boulder, CO: Sounds True, 2010.

McTaggart, Lynne. *The Field: The Quest for the Secret Force of the Universe*. New York: Harper Collins, 2008.

McTaggart, Lynne. *The Power of Eight: Harnessing the Miraculous Energies of a Small Group to Heal Others, Your Life, and the World*. New York: Atria, 2018.

Osbon, Diane K. *Reflections on the Art of Living: A Joseph Campbell Companion*. New York: Harper Perennial, 1991.

Piaget, Jean. *The Origins of Intelligence in Children.* Translated by Margaret Cook. New York, NY: International University Press, 1952.

Ray, Reginald A. *Somatic Descent: Experiencing the Ultimate Intelligence of the Body.* Audio CDs. Boulder, CO: Sounds True, 2016.

Robbins, Anthony. *Notes from a Friend: A Quick and Simple Guide to Taking Charge of Your Life.* Great Britain: Pocket Books, 2001.

Robbins, Anthony. *Awaken the Giant Within: How to Take Immediate Control of Your Mental, Emotional, Physical and Financial Destiny.* New York: Simon & Shuster, 2013.

Rosenberg, Marshall B. *Nonviolent Communication: A Language of Life.* Encinitas, CA: PuddleDancer Press, 2nd Edition, 2003.

Rosenberg, Marshall B. *Living Nonviolent Communication; Practical Tools to Connect and Communicate Skillfully in Every Situation.* Boulder, CO: Sounds True, 2012.

Schwartz, Richard, C. *Introduction to the Internal Family Systems Model.* Oak Park, IL: Trailheads Publications, 2001.

Sharma, Robin. *The Monk Who Sold His Ferrari: A Fable About Fulfilling Your Dreams & Reaching Your Destiny.* New York: Harper Collins, 1999.

Simon, Tami, ed. *The Self-Acceptance Project: How to be Kind & Compassionate Towards Yourself in Any Situation.* Boulder, CO: Sounds True, 2016.

Singer, Michael A. *The Untethered Soul: The Journey Beyond Yourself.* Oakland, CA: New Harbinger, 2007.

Singer, Michael A. *The Surrender Experiment: My Journey into Life's Perfection*. New York: Harmony Books, 2015.

Taylor, Steve. *The Meaning: Poetic and Spiritual Reflections*. Winchester, UK: O-Books, 2012.

Taylor, Steve. *The Calm Center*. Novato, CA: The World Library, 2015.

The Comprehensive Addiction and Recovery Act (CARA). *Public Law 114-198*. (Original Bills as Introduced in 114th Congress: S.524/H.R.953). https://www.cadca.org/comprehensive-addiction-and-recovery-act-cara

The Self-Acceptance Summit: How to Overcome Self-Judgement and Live Life of Bravery, Compassion and Authenticity. Sounds True. http://self-acceptance-summit-sfm.soundstrue.com/

Tift, Bruce. *Already Free: Buddhism Meets Psychotherapy on the Path of Liberation*. Boulder, CO: Sounds True, 2015.

Tolle, Eckhart. *The Power of Now: A Guide to Spiritual Enlightenment*. Audio CD. Novato, CA: New World Library, 1999.

Tolle, Eckhart. *Stillness Speaks*. Novato, CA: New World Library, 2003.

Tolle, Eckhart. *A New Earth: Awakening to Your Life's Purpose*. England: Penguin Group, 2005.

Ware, Bronnie. *The Top Five Regrets of the Dying: A Life Transformed by the Dearly Departing*. Carlsbad, CA: Hay House, 2012.

Watts, Alan. *Become What You Are*. Boston: Shambhala Publications, 2003.

Waylon, Mark. *It Didn't Start with You: How Inherited Family Trauma Shapes Who We Are and How to End the Cycle*. New York: Penguin Random House, 2016.

Wilber, Ken. *A Brief History of Everything.* Boulder: Shambhala Publications. 2017

Williams, Russel. *Not I, Not Other than I: The Life and Teachings of Russel Williams.* Edited by Steve Taylor. Winchester, UK: O-Books, 2015.

About the Author

Angela Silva Mendes' diverse academic background includes bachelor's degrees in education and communication theories, and a master's in international affairs. Guided by her value to serve and her thirst for meaning, Angela also holds a range of personal development certificates including neuro-linguistics programming, mindfulness, and coaching. Honoring her African heritage, Angela named her practice Upanji, meaning energy, a space of acceptance, holding what arises, and integration. With work experience in Europe, Africa, and the USA, Angela coaches, facilitates, and teaches internationally through individual sessions, workshops, and talks. She believes that self-work, based on embodied awareness, is a crucial vehicle for social justice. www.upanji.com.

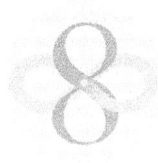

Notes

1. Many authors and teachers have supported my understanding in the distinctions between physical pain and emotional pain but it was with Adyashanti, Chodron, and Brach that I took this knowledge to practice.
2. Pareto Analysis Using Pareto Principle (80/20 rule), Visual Paradigm Online May 1st 2021 https://online.visual-paradigm.com/knowledge/pareto-chart/pareto-analysis-using-pareto-principle-20-80-rules/.
3. Van Der Leeuw, J. J. 1928. The Conquest of Illusion. p. 9. Wheaton, IL Theosophical Publishing House.
4. Before I did my coaching certification I attended a few workshops and read some books about the subject. These are just a few, Brendon, Buckingham, Covey, Hill, Howard, Kiosaki, Robbins, Sharma, Tracy.
5. I love De Mello's concept that infinity only means timeless—no time therefore it is right now, *Here*.

6. After reading Eckhart Tolle's books I attended his retreat where I asked Can we Support others? His answer, you can watch on his youtube page was, yes presence. https://www.youtube.com/watch?v=dP7a8aIfDaY.

7. The first time I had the courage to see my illusions of control was while reading Brown, Brené. *I Thought It Was Just Me (but it isn't): Telling the Truth about Perfectionism, Inadequacy, and Power.* Followed by *The Gifts of Imperfection: Let Go of Who You Think You're Supposed to Be and Embrace Who You Are.* And *Daring Greatly: How the Courage to Be Vulnerable Transforms the Way We Live, Love, Parent, and Lead.* Any of Brown's work tackles this widespread problem with the same invitation.

8. Kahneman, Daniel. *Thinking, Fast and Slow.* New York: Farrar, Straus and Giroux, 2013.

9. Baer, Drake. "Kahneman: Your Cognitive Biases Act Like Optical Illusions." The Cut. January 13, 2017.

10. Although some like Braden in *Fractal Time* discuss time as cyclical and not linear.

11. There is a great deal in the market about the power of intention and Lynn McTaggart has even got scientists to do some experiments to prove this.

12. Our beliefs have power this is what Bruce Lipton explains in his book *The Biology of Belief.*

13. Thomas H. Holmes and Richard H. Rahe, "The Social Readjustment Rating Scale." *Journal of Psychosomatic Research*, 11, no. 2 (August 1967): 213–218.

14. Jean Piaget, *The Origins of Intelligence in Children,* trans. Margaret Cook (New York, NY: International University Press, 1952).

15. The work of *Waylon, Mark. It Didn't Start with You: How Inherited Family Trauma Shapes Who We Are and How to End the Cycle. New York: Penguin Random House, 2016.* the book is about family trauma but it is a wake up call to how much we carry in ourselves even before we are consciously aware.

16. The Comprehensive Addiction and Recovery Act (CARA). *Public Law 114-198.* (Original Bills as Introduced in 114th Congress: S.524/H.R.953).

17. Arnold Ventures. "Evidence Based Strategies for Abatement of Harms from the Opioid Epidemic." Carnevale Associates LLC. November 10, 2020.

18. If you are curious about neuroplasticity start with The Brain That Changes Itself by Doidge, Norman.

19. This quote is famous but it is worded slightly different, "The very cave you are afraid to enter turns out to be the source of what you are looking for." as recorded by Osbon, Diane K. Reflections on the Art of Living: A Joseph Campbell Companion. New York: Harper Perennial, 1991.

20. Adam Auton et al., "A Global Reference for Human Genetic Variation," *Nature* 526, no. 7571 (2015): 68–74.

21. Attul Atewand, in his book *Being Mortal: Medicine and What Matters in the End*, asks us to have the difficult conversations and why it is important to understand that life is not only about extending time alone, but it is what constitutes quality of life for each person.

22. Karla McLaren in her book *The Language of Emotions: What Your Feelings are Trying to Tell You* does an excellent job in guiding us through.

23. Kahneman, Daniel. Thinking, Fast and Slow. New York: Farrar, Straus and Giroux, 2013.

24. Sharma, Robin. *How Champions Are Made.* https://www.robinsharma.com/article/ how-champions-are-made.
25. Supported greatly by the works of Simon through Sounds True.
26. Regardless of the inherited perceptions, experiences and anxieties Bruce Tift's book title *Already Free* defends that the freedom we seek is already available.
27. There a universe inside ourselves and Singer's work supported me in this exploration.
28. Levine, Peter. *Waking the Tiger: Healing Trauma, The Innate Capacity to Transform Overwhelming Experiences.* Berkley, CA: North Atlantic Books, 1997.
29. Marshall Rosenberg's Non-Violent Communication can be applied to ourselves as well.
30. Levine, Peter A. Waking the Tiger: Healing Trauma, The Innate Capacity to Transform Overwhelming Experiences. Berkley, CA: North Atlantic Books, 1997.
31. This combines both Levine's Somatic Experiencing and Schwartz, Internal Family System, accounts of this search for wholeness.

www.ingramcontent.com/pod-product-compliance
Lightning Source LLC
Chambersburg PA
CBHW041929090426
42744CB00016B/1990